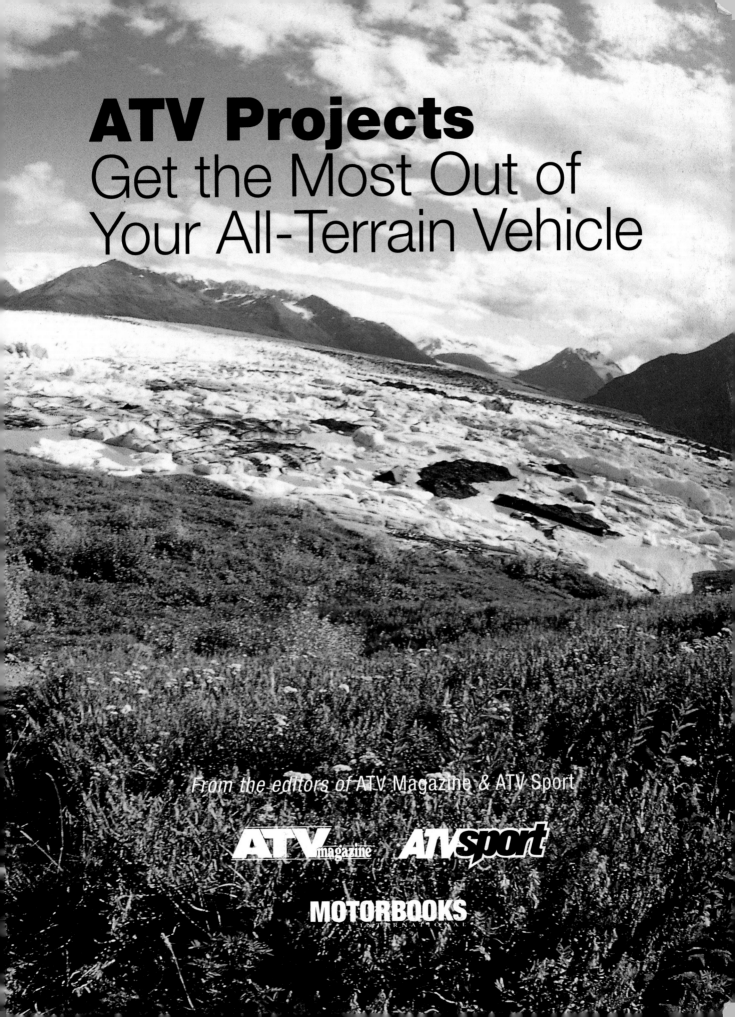

# ATV Projects
## Get the Most Out of Your All-Terrain Vehicle

*From the editors of ATV Magazine & ATV Sport*

**ATV**magazine  **ATV**sport

**MOTORBOOKS**
INTERNATIONAL

First published in 2004 by Motorbooks International, an imprint of MBI Publishing Company, Galtier Plaza, Suite 200, 380 Jackson Street, St. Paul, MN 55101-3885 USA

Motorbooks International titles are also available at discounts in bulk quantity for industrial or sales-promotional use. For details write to Special Sales Manager at Motorbooks International Wholesalers & Distributors, Galtier Plaza, Suite 200, 380 Jackson Street, St. Paul, MN 55101-3885 USA.

*ATV Magazine* and *ATV Sport* are registered trademarks of Ehlert Publishing Group and are used with permission. Copyright © 2004 Ehlert Publishing Group. All rights reserved. For further information regarding these magazines, please visit the following Web sites: www.atvmagonline.com and www.atvsport.com.

ISBN 0-7603-2058-6

**On the cover, main:** A hunting-equipped ATV sporting a mounted gun holder and camouflaged storage bag. *Lee Klancher*

**Inset:** Brake replacement is often necessary once you've put a few trail miles on your quad.

**On the frontispiece:** The number of ATV riders has skyrocketed in the last few years as the sport has become known as a great recreational hobby and as a way to get farming and landscaping work done very efficiently. *Mike Haenggi*

**On the title page:** When out on an ATV ride, you are to be surrounded by nature and great views, such as this one in Alaska. *Lee Klancher*

**On the back cover:** A rider checks out how well his ATV-mounted mower is trimming the grass on this lawn.

Edited by Leah Noel
Designed by Kou Lor

Printed in China

# Contents

# Introduction

Seeing nature firsthand, buzzing past trees that are hundreds of years old, traversing an awe-inspiring stream that is far off the beaten path. For those who love to get on an ATV and head out to the back country, these experiences are just part of what makes ATV riding special. Such bliss can also be found on the racetrack, zipping around a dirt course and hitting a double jump to get a bird's-eye view of the track from 30 feet in the air. On the other hand, many ATV riders use their quads for plowing farm fields, rounding up cattle, and hauling landscaping equipment.

ATVs can be used in a lot of different applications; we can play and work on the same machine year-round. Because ATVs are often used for hard work and hard play, maintaining them is essential. That's part of the reason for this book. Whether your quad is a worker or a player, or both, there's something in these pages that will speak to you about keeping your machine in tip-top shape. What happens when the showroom quality of your ATV isn't enough, or when that quality dips slightly because the brakes are fading? You need to know how to fix

For those who love the great outdoors, ATV riding can provide the perfect way to get out and explore places that are off the beaten path.

your quad, alter it, and adjust it to make it perfect for you.

So if your ATV's suspension needs to be plusher, or you'd like to know how to properly and safely trailer your machine, keep reading—this collection of projects from *ATV Magazine* and *ATV Sport* addresses both of these issues and many more. Through these projects, you'll be able to see the progression in the sport of ATVing, along with the progression of the machines being produced.

Through all of the changes in the industry in the last 10 years, we at *ATV Magazine* and *ATV Sport* have been there. We've seen sport quads make a comeback after being long ignored by the major manufacturers. We've seen the engine-displacement size of ATVs go from 400 ccs to 750 ccs. We've seen electronic fuel injection replace carburetors, four-stroke thumpers replace two-stroke engines, and electronic readouts with GPS systems appear on consoles were there were none before. The changes are constant and so exciting that we can barely contain our joy when a new machine is introduced to us.

We've dedicated our waking hours to this growing sport, and we hope you enjoy this book as much as we enjoy writing about and riding ATVs. It's our passion, and because you're reading this, we know it's your passion too.

—the staff of *ATV Magazine* and *ATV Sport*

**Above:** ATVs aren't just for play, though. They make great work horses, helping mow, plow, and plant your lawn and garden.

**Right:** Hunters also are big ATV fans as quads provide a fast way to move from hunting spot to hunting spot.

# Tool Essentials for the Trail

When it comes to ATV riding, the most important tools to have are the ones you bring along with you on the trail. That's where you really do need to be pretty self-reliant. By carrying the right goodies, you can save a lot of hassle on a day trip, and having these tools is essential when you are riding into serious wilderness. So here's a list of the things that can help get you home, or at least make your day more pleasant:

(Note: All of these can be fit into a backpack, but you probably want to put them in a waterproof storage box that is mounted to your rack. This list is also pretty extensive, so you can lighten up for shorter rides.)

## Main Tools
- Combination wrenches (8/10 millimeters, 12/14 millimeters, 17/19 millimeters)
- A reversible screwdriver
- Allen wrenches (2 millimeter, 2.5 millimeter, 3 millimeter, 4 millimeter, 5 millimeter, 6 millimeter, 8 millimeter, 10 millimeter)
- A plug wrench (specific to bike)
- Axle wrenches (specific to bike)
- Tire irons
- Leatherman

## Bonus Tools
- A small Vise-Grip (doubles as shift lever in a pinch)
- A small file
- A spoke wrench
- A 1/4-inch drive socket wrench
- Deep-well six-point sockets (8 millimeter, 10 millimeter, 12 millimeter)

## Bonus Repair Stuff
- Duct tape
- Safety wire
- Small hose clamps
- Quick-set epoxy

## Spares
- A front tube (works for rear)
- A master link
- Common fasteners (8 millimeter, 10 millimeter, 12 millimeter)

## Bonus Spares
- A pre-oiled air filter
- A quart of crankcase oil
- A small can of silicone lube

## Miscellaneous
- Water bladders (These can be strapped to a pack, or use a pack with an integral water container.)
- Three to four PowerBars (for that on-trail energy boost)
- A bandana (for wiping goggles and for use as a makeshift facemask)
- A good map
- A compass
- Packable rain gear
- A cheap, compact space blanket (light ones available at outdoor stores)
- Sandals (cheap flip-flops work well)
- Clean socks, gloves, underwear, shorts, and a T-shirt in a sealable plastic bag

If you have a box that's always packed with your trail tools and supplies, you'll make getting out the door for a ride that much easier. *Lee Klancher*

**Above and right:** Once out on the trail, you never know when you might need to break that box open and do some wrenching. *Lee Klancher*

- A fleece shirt and long johns (for cooler climates only)
- Matches or lighter
- ID, credit card, local bills ($50–100 US)
- Duct tape (always a must)
- Two dozen sheets of toilet paper in sealable plastic bag
- Zip ties, various sizes (These fix ANYTHING.)
- A tow rope/strap
- Spare sealable plastic bags
- A flat fix kit
- Five-minute epoxy
- Clear goggle lens (use tinted in daylight)
- A headlamp (Petzl Tikka is light, compact, and cheap.)
- A tow strap
- A tow chain, shackles, and clevis (if your ATV is equipped with a winch)
- An axe and shovel
- A basic first aid kit

—Lee Klancher

# SECTION 1
# ON THE JOB

| PROJECT 1 | Cleaning up Shop |
|---|---|

Staff Report

**Time:** Pit Pal: 30 minutes to an hour; Pour-N-Restore: 15–20 minute application, overnight drying

**Tools:** Pit Pal: drill, rivet gun, level, drill bits; Pour-N-Restore: broom, fan

**Talent:** Pit Pal: ★★★; Pour-N-Restore: ★

**Tab:** Anywhere between $6.99 to $155

**Parts:** Rivets, Pit Pal products

**Benefit:** Organization is key

**Complementary Project:** Creating the ultimate trailer or shop

Shakespeare once wrote: "In every mess have folly and the feeders." Well, the shop here at *ATV Magazine* headquarters has a tendency to be a folly for the feeders. It sometimes needs help—cans of contact cleaner, paper towel rolls, and half-full oil containers can crowd every nook and cranny. The trailer at the shop can be equally as disorganized—when it is being used. Things that should be on shelving often are scattered about the enclosure—rolling around the trailer with each turn. One time, a quart of oil exploded in the trailer while en route to an event; it wasn't pretty. Is your shop any better? If it isn't, you can make it a more productive working environment. Here's how.

Here are some Pit Pal products securely riveted to a trailer's walls. These products are simple to install and will come in handy for years.

## Pit Pal

Friendly name, huh? Pit Pal has long served the needs of many a car racer. Its products are well known among stock car circles as being quality items that no self-respecting racer or shop owner would do without. Pit Pal makes organization in both the shop and trailer a breeze with a line of simple, yet wonderful, aluminum-constructed products.

Its trailer door cabinet ($155) is awash in features that every trailer needs. It is designed to attach to any trailer door that is at least 25 inches wide and 30 inches high. To install the cabinet, drill pilot holes through it and then rivet the item to support rails within the trailer door. To ensure that the cabinet will hold when loaded, use heavy-duty rivets.

Pit Pal's trailer door cabinet holds everything you might need and features a lockable fold-down tray (top). Under the tray is a bar that can hold two rolls of paper towels (above).

The cabinet has a lot of places to store things, including a fold-down table that is handy for holding any items—such as tools or parts—that you might need. Underneath the cabinet is space for two rolls of paper towels. And to prevent the towels from unraveling, Pit Pal includes its locking pin washer kit too. Each shelf is big enough to hold nine aerosol spray cans. But the shelves can hold pretty much anything, including cleaning products and other small items that often are missing in action in a busy shop.

Pit Pal's double bay helmet shelf ($100) is a must for anyone who trailers machines in an enclosed trailer. If nothing else, the shelf keeps things tidy in the trailer. It has 12 hanger spots for gear, jackets, pullovers, etc. In fact, if you stretch a couple of bungee nets into the bays, you could probably keep your helmets here permanently. You could also cut the rubber matting to fit the bottom of the helmet storage spaces to prevent your lids from rattling around. The 28.25- x 15- x 12-inch shelf provides ample storage. Pit Pal also makes single-helmet bays and three-helmet bays.

The double bay helmet shelf not only has space for a pair of helmets, but has spots for 12 hangers underneath.

Finally, Pit Pal offers deluxe air brackets ($31). These can be used things to hold, among other things, air and garden hoses. Included in the deluxe model is a small shelf that holds anything from an air gauge to small tools. The shelf also is handy for holding items that you may need while working on an ATV in the trailer.

### Pour-N-Restore

When the mess in your shop includes a nasty stain, a product called Pour-N-Restore can help make your working area pristine again. Pour-N-Restore has a long list of stains it will remove: motor oil, grease, hydraulic fluid, coolant, brake fluid, transmission fluid, synthetic oils, food grease from animal fats, cooking oil, tar, citronella oil, and wax. Pour-N-Restore is also advertised to work on various concrete and masonry surfaces, including exposed aggregate, patio blocks, paving bricks, quarry tile, stone, and colored concrete. It will not, however, work on asphalt.

Here are the directions: Open bottle and pour. Simple, effective, easy. But in temperatures above 60 degrees Fahrenheit, expect to wait at least five to eight hours before the substance is completely dry and ready to be swept away. That's right, swept. Pour-N-Restore dries to a powder that absorbs the stain from the surface. If the temperature is below 60 degrees, dry time is considerably lengthened. A fan can be used to aid drying. The product also needs to be used in a well-ventilated environment. Since *ATV Magazine*'s shop is in Minnesota, the temp was below 60 degrees when we tried it, and the Pour-N-Restore needed to dry over a weekend. When the floor finally was swept after the treatment we nearly wept—the stain was gone. The best part was that this product is enviro-friendly, so Pour-N-Restore can be disposed of without worrying about washing harmful cleanser down the drain. Pour-N-Restore also is citrus-based, so the smell isn't harsh, overpowering, or chemical.

For stubborn stains that are not removed with the first application, apply again and scrub the stained area.

See that nasty stain next to the bottle? It doesn't exist anymore.

<table>
<tr><td>

# PROJECT 2

</td><td>

# Working with an Air Lift

</td></tr>
</table>

Staff Report

**Time:** 1.5 hours

**Tools:** Air compressor, ratchet driver, sockets

**Talent:** ★★★

**Tab:** $900

**Tip:** Make sure you have enough room in the shop for this lift

**Benefit:** Makes working on projects easier

**Complementary Project:** Shop organization

Now that your shop is organized, it's time to get working. But for jobs such as adjusting valves, changing belts, and changing oil, you usually end up bending over your ATV or kneeling on concrete for extended periods of time. And sooner or later, after performing many of these tasks, you realize that concrete truly is not forgiving and your back isn't meant to bend awkwardly for hours.

In an effort to solve this problem, those of us at *ATV Magazine* have tried using manual ATV lifts that cranked up, but found them to be slow. They also didn't lift the machine high enough for some jobs. If only you could rig some sort of winching system that would suspend the ATV from your shop's ceiling. On second thought, that could be a disaster in the making. Thankfully, there is a better solution.

The Handy Air Lift in action. Here, it is raised to its 30-inch working height. When compressed, it is only 7 inches high.

The foot pedal is easy to use and connects in the air line between the lift and air compressor.

The ramp on the back of the lift is full width and makes driving machines on and off the lift a breeze.

The Handy Air Lift ($729) from Handy Industries is heavy—Handy lists it as weighing 304 pounds. But heavy is good, right? Doesn't heavy mean heavy-duty? With its powder-coated, solid-steel construction, this lift is just that.

Another reason it's so heavy-duty? How about a lifting capacity of 1,000 pounds? Think about it—the Handy Air Lift can hoist 1,000 pounds 30 inches high on its 80- x 24-inch deck. While 24 inches may not be wide enough to support an ATV, even the widest ATV can fit on the deck with Handy Industries' 12-inch side extensions ($175). With the extensions added on each side, the width of the lift is 48 inches. This width also allows you to work on your snowmobiles in the winter.

The lift is operated via a foot pedal, which is connected to the air line and runs from our shop's compressor. Operation is simple: Depress the lever one way to lift; depress it the opposite way to lower. Once raised, the lift has a safety bar to prevent the deck from falling. Since the lift is operated by air pressure, a little bleed-off happens when the lift stops, and the deck eventually lowers on its own from the weight of the ATV. With the lock bar, however, that does not happen. The lock bar fits into teeth that lock the deck at different heights. Plus, once the lift is locked, you can unhook its air line to use an impact wrench or other pneumatic tool.

When compressed, the lift is a mere seven inches high, so it will fit under a car or truck in the garage. A ramp making up one side of its deck allows ATVs to easily travel up it. Beneath the decking, the carriage has wheels so it can easily "scissor" up to the desired height.

The lift also does not need much of a compressor tank to operate; a 5 horsepower compressor does the job easily. Handy recommends 6.7 cfm at 100 psi. If you do not want to run the lift off a compressor, Handy Industries also has an electric version available for $210 more. The company also makes several add-ons for the lift, including a wheel clamp for motorcycles, snowmobile wings, trike extensions, and more.

If you have any water in your compressor's tank, you'll find out when you use this lift. After being left idle through the winter, *ATV Magazine*'s compressor was not drained properly. On the lift's maiden voyage, the water blew out of the pedal in the form of a greasy, yellow substance. Bleech! After cleaning the shop floor, we'll never make that mistake again.

Adding an air lift to your shop isn't for everyone. But, if you do lots of maintenance on your machines, or have several different machines that you work on, it will be a welcome addition. Plus, it will last a lifetime in a home shop setting.

# PROJECT 3 | Mounting & Inflating Tires

Staff Report

**Time:** 30 minutes per tire

**Tools:** Tire irons, air compressor, soapy water

**Talent:** ★★★★

**Tab:** N/A

**Parts:** Tires, wheels

**Tip:** Be patient

**Benefit:** Save money

**Complementary Project:** Changing brake pads or shoes

If you mount your own tires, pay careful attention—seating new tires on their beads presents many serious dangers. While these low-pressure tires are usually designed to run between 3 and 5 pounds of pressure, much more pressure than that is needed to actually seat the tire on the rim.

During normal operation, ATVs place heavy side loads on the tires, especially during cornering maneuvers. With relatively little air pressure to keep tires properly seated on the rims, the tires' beads must fit very snugly against the wheels' beads seats. This force-fit keeps the tires from peeling off the rims and going flat during radical maneuvers.

The downside of the snug fit is that it makes the tire mounting significantly more difficult. Pressures between 15 and 20 pounds are often needed to properly

Mounting new tires requires higher than normal pressures to "snap" the bead into position. *Lee Klancher*

seat new tires. Since these tires are flexible, there's a slim chance the tire could explode and cause serious injury during this procedure if you do not use the proper tools and safety precautions.

Donny Meyers at Douglas Wheel offers these basic tips and proper mounting instructions:

First, replace the valve stem before mounting a new tire. This is cheap insurance. Old valves rot and leak or blow out.

Then, when seating new tires, always use a clip-on style air chuck with a long extension hose, remote filler, and inflating gauge. Meyers recommends placing the tire behind a cinder block wall or under a trailer when seating the bead. With the gauge on a remote filler hose, your tire should be in your line of sight. If the tire explodes, you would be safely out of the way.

Use a tire-mounting lubricant if necessary. This allows the tire to seat more easily. Lube the tire, rim, and bead seat. Meyers recommends using soap and water, glass cleaner, or another non-oil based product as a lubricant. You will want to use something that evaporates and doesn't leave an oily film, which would allow the tire to turn on the rim.

Also, before inflating the tire, remove the valve core. This allows the air to be released very rapidly after the tire has been seated. Never stand over the tire and hold the valve stem to release the air. The air pressure drops slowly and the tire could explode before you get it down to a safe pressure.

## Stubborn Tires

Some people also inflate stubborn tires and leave them lying around the garage floor until the bead seats. This is not a safe practice. If the tire exploded when a bystander was next to it or if the bead were to seat when a bystander had his fingers on the tire's seat, he could be severely injured.

To make tire mounting easier, you may want to let the tire sit out in the sun for a while. Meyers says that the sun warms the tire and makes it more flexible, which makes the tire easier to seat.

Inflate the tire until you hear the bead seats snap, or until you reach the manufacturer's maximum inflation pressure. Never exceed this pressure. If the bead does not seat by the time you reach the maximum recommended tire pressure, release all air from the tire/wheel assembly.

At this point, Meyers recommends wrapping a tie-down strap around the inner belly of the tire. Then pull the tie-down strap tight. Inflate the tire with air. The tie-down strap will keep the tire from flexing and will help the bead seat more easily. Again, do not exceed the tire manufacturer's recommended tire pressure. If the tire still does not seat, contact your tire wheel supplier for help.

Once the tire's bead is properly seated, disconnect the air chuck and let all the air out of the tire. Re-install the valve core and inflate it to the proper operating pressure.

# PROJECT 4 | Choosing & Using a Mower

By Glenn Hansen, Blake Stranz, and Chaz Rice

**Time:** As long as it takes to find the one you want

**Tools:** Your brain

**Talent:** ★★

**Tab:** $200 and up

**Tip:** Choose the right size for your needs

**Benefit:** Makes cutting grass fun and easy

**Complementary Project:** Shopping for other implements for your ATV

Weeds have overtaken your yard; everything in sight is overgrown and looking like it could conquer the world (or at least your neighbor's) at any moment. Without question, it's time to do some major mowing. But what if you don't have a mower that can handle this Herculean task? Or what if you need something that will move dirt and grass? Or make a clear-cut path through your land? Well, the market is full of mower options for ATVs. Below are some of the models that those of us at *ATV Magazine*

have tested and feel are worth considering if you have a lot of yardwork to do.

## Quad-Cut 58 Mower

Nobody likes cutting grass. Max Swisher of rural Missouri didn't, yet he turned his distaste for the activity into a big lawn care business—one so successful that his son Wayne has expanded it in recent years. As part of that expansion, the Swisher company manufactures a lot of mowers that work in combination with an ATV.

Convert your ATV into a riding lawn mower with Swisher's Quad Cut 58.

Controls for the Quad-Cut's power, blade engagement, and ignition mount to the rear rack.

One such product is the Quad-Cut 58, which consists of several parts. Using a hitch pin, the 16-horsepower engine unit mounts to the rear of the ATV and rides on a single caster. Drive is directed to the cutting deck via a shaft. The engine starts through a rear rack–mounted console, which also controls the power of the engine and blade engagement; the engine features an electric start. With the auxiliary engine attached to the ATV, one simply has to roll the ATV over the deck and attach the deck to the engine and bracket. In all, the process takes less than five minutes.

With a turn of the key, the mower's engine comes to life and the blades engage. These blades span the mower's 58-inch cutting deck, which can be raised for high-speed transport.

When you're first using this mower, you quickly discover the benefits of mounting it underneath an ATV, rather than towing it. Control of the unit is precise and the cutting deck goes exactly where the driver wants it to go. Backing up is even easier because you don't have to worry about the trailing arm of a pull-behind mower. The wide cut also does not require you to go over spots where the ATV tires have matted down the grass.

There is a little push in the front end when you make corners while using the Quad-Cut. The heavy auxiliary engine sits on the rear hitch, lightening the front end, but additional weight on the handlebars

helps the front tires stay on the ground. On more challenging terrain, the mower still moves well. Its weight lowers the quad's center of gravity, so mowing hillsides is a snap.

### Swisher Rough Cut

The Swisher Rough Cut mower is 44 inches wide and can cut a basic trail in a single pass. In two passes, you can create nearly an 8-foot-wide trail quickly and efficiently with this mower.

### Set It up

The unit weighs nearly 500 pounds and a utility trailer is probably the best bet for transporting it. A full-size pickup could hold it as well, but loading the mower into the bed could be a chore.

For the most part, the mower is assembled at the factory. All the customer needs to do is attach the hitch bar to the mower and install the swivel hitch to the ATV. Then, the hitch is connected to the ATV's ball mount. If you currently use a ball with your ATV, you will have to remove it to hook up the Swisher mower; this is kind of a pain.

Assembling the mower is straightforward. Simply bolt the hitch bar in the center of the front torsion bar for a straight pull, or bolt the hitch bar to the right or left edge for offset mowing. Swisher recommends offset mowing so the tow vehicle doesn't trample the grass before the mower gets to it. A large crank sets the mower height to the desired level. Once the height is set, bolt the "L" hitch to the hitch bar so that the mower deck rides level to the ground. It's easiest to set the mower up on a hard, flat surface, like a garage floor.

The blade engage/disengage lever connects to the rear rack with three bolts. The racks on our 2004 Yamaha Grizzly didn't offer enough depth, and the bolts bottomed out before the mounting plate was tight, so we had to add larger nuts as spacers to secure the lever's mounting plate.

### Ready to Mow

With the unit assembled and attached to the ATV, you're almost ready to gas and go. First, though, Swisher recommends a short, five-minute break-in on the mower. Start by parking the ATV with the mower connected. Then fire up the mower engine and let it idle. Slowly engage the drive belt and let the mower run for five minutes.

Now, you're ready to mow. The mower works best at slow speeds, and Swisher doesn't recommend mowing faster than five miles per hour. This can pose a challenge, especially on big bore ATVs. On a Grizzly, five miles per hour is barely above idle.

As you can see, the weeds and grass at the R&D center were completely overgrown.

As for cutting effectiveness, the mower does well. If the weeds and grass you're mowing are thick and more than four feet tall, you'll need to slow the mower to a crawl, so the grass can have time to spring back into the spinning blade after being bent down under the mower's front edge.

The 10.5-horsepower Briggs & Stratton engine provides plenty of power to the blades, especially when mowing thick grass. However, that many ponies running full bore sucks a lot of gas, so when using this mower on a tough job, carry a gas can on the ATV racks so you can fill up the Rough Cut when it runs dry.

Due to the length of the grass, there was a bit of "spring up" that required a second pass with the Swisher Rough Cut.

Level the deck on a flat surface to make certain the mower cuts properly.

The heavy-duty steel deck offers a feeling of confidence, even when the mower encounters hard objects, such as rocks or chunks of wood. You hear the items clank under the deck, but the mower doesn't let them escape. Still, you should wear a helmet and eye protection when using this product.

When you cut low to the ground, disengage the blades when you go over small hills, bumps, or swales. This will prevent the blades from bottoming out on the dirt. The tires track nicely, and a steel bar guides weeds and rocks out of the path of the mower so that the deck does not wander or lift off the ground.

At $1,500, the RT-44 mower is not inexpensive. But it is a solid unit that should last a long time, and if you have rough mowing to do, it will do the job expertly.

## 44-Inch Rugged Cut Trailcutter

This is a pull-behind rough cut mower that does cut just about anything. During a test at Swisher headquarters, this mower chopped down a lot of brush and small trees even though it had a dull blade.

The true sign of a good pull-behind mower, though, is the sound it makes while chopping brush. If the engine is underpowered, it will bog when getting into the thick stuff. The 10.5-horsepower Tecumseh engine did bog a couple of times during testing, but almost any engine would in this type of situation. When the engine did bog, it was hung up on a tree that was just a little out of the cutting range of the 44-Inch Rugged Cut Trailcutter. A sharp blade would maybe change things a bit.

## 50-Inch ATV Plow

There are ATV-mounted plows, and then there is the Swisher ATV-mounted plow. The designers at Swisher set out to make a heavy-duty plow to move snow and dirt, and by all accounts they've succeeded.

First off, you'll love how this plow mounts to your ATV. Instead of the usual mounting plate that requires you to get on the ground in order to slide pins into it, this plow uses an ATV's hitch. A collapsible shaft runs from the front of the plow to the ATV hitch and mounts via a receiver hitch. This, according to Swisher,

Clear a path through the worst of the brush with the Rugged Cut 44-inch pull-behind mower.

This is one of the most heavy-duty plows around.

allows the plow to be raised higher than other plow units on the market.

Changing the blade angle is inventive as well. A rope runs from the pin, which sets the blade angle to the ATV operator. A quick pull of the rope releases the pin and allows the blade angle to change.

This plow handles everything: gravel, sand, snow, and feed. You name it, the plow can take it. When other plows fail because the load is too great for the trip springs, the Swisher plow keeps plowing. The reason for this plow's abusive power comes from its rugged construction. Anywhere a plow could be reinforced has been reinforced on this model; nothing has been skimped. The plow mount is constructed of 1/8-inch powder-coated steel; the reinforced blade is constructed from the same stock.

Now for the downside of this ruggedness—the plow weighs as much as the ATV! Well, maybe not that much, but enough to compress the MacPherson struts on the Polaris Sportsman 500 ATV with which we tested the plow. While the plow might offer longer vertical travel, any advantage over other plows is lost due to front suspension compression. Plus, the weight of the plow will strain most winches over time. Only a long-term comparison will tell if the plow needs to be so heavy.

## AcrEase Rough Cut Mower

In thick and heavy bush, this mower can power through obstacle after obstacle, leaving a clear-cut path in its wake.

Get a rough cut mower through this terrain?  With the AcrEase Rough Cut, that's possible.

Heavy-gauge steel and a high-horsepower engine make this a durable and strong mower.

The AcrEase 55-Inch Rough Cut Mower is built by Kunz Engineering of Mendota, Illinois. This company is also home to AcrEase Wing Mowers, which are built for finishing jobs. In prior tests of the AcrEase Wing Mowers, designed by Gary Kunz, we were impressed with both the quality of their final cut and their maneuverability. For the AcrEase Rough Cut test, we chose a coworker's "rough" backyard as the ideal testing ground.

### Finesse in the Rough

When using this mower, you will instantly notice how light the 515-pound AcrEase feels. The mower's four pneumatic tires carry its weight well and make the unit easy enough for any ATV to pull.

The beauty of this mower, though, is its versatility and surprising finesse. The AcrEase Rough Cut hitches to your ATV in several different ways, including being pulled straight behind an ATV (we used a Honda Rubicon). This setup can make it difficult to look behind and see the mower, but since it is right behind the ATV, you shouldn't need to look back.

On the test, the Honda and AcrEase Rough Cut made a lot of handlebar turns, snaking through the trees of a small, rough plot. Still the mower handled it all with ease. Only once or twice did the ATV need to be put in reverse. When it did back up, little effort was needed to do this successfully.

Pull the mower off to the side for mowing under trees or along shorelines.

This tree trimmed down to size quickly. The mower's maneuverability is enhanced by its hitch.

And like all AcrEase mowers, the AcrEase Rough Cut is easily pulled off to the side of the ATV for mowing ditches, shorelines, fence rows, or other hard-to-reach spots. Its low-profile construction lets it cut under trees and low-hanging branches. Kunz designed the mower's hitch and the front caster tires for that kind of versatility.

### Mow 'Em Down

But can it mow? The lot was full of thick grass, which was up to four feet tall. Hidden in this mess were several small trees and brush. The AcrEase Rough Cut handled the thick mess without problem. Even a tree that was about two inches around came down easily under this mower's big blades.

Beneath that 10-gauge steel deck are two 30-inch mower blades. Powering the blades is a 17-horsepower Tecumseh with overhead valves and electric start. It uses a manual blade-engagement clutch. The cutting height is adjustable from two to eight inches above ground. Two manual cranks, one on each side of the deck, easily raise or lower the unit.

The Rough Cut also includes all the necessary safety features, including a noncutting safety area near the edges of the deck. The mower's blades are protected from rocks by heavy-gauge steel on the intake side of the deck.

<table>
<tr><td>

# PROJECT 5

</td><td>

# Plowing Soil

</td></tr>
</table>

By Glenn Hansen

**Time:** 30 minutes to 2 hours

**Tools:** Plow, ATV

**Talent:** ★★

**Tab:** Weekend Warrior disc retails for $1,259

**Tip:** This turns ATV riding into legitimate work

**Benefit:** Working the land is a lot easier with an ATV

If you've got a stretch of grass and weeds that hasn't been turned upside down since the Ice Age, you're going to need a chisel plow to fully till that soil for planting your garden or small crop.

And if you don't want to spend an eternity getting this project done, you should use an ATV-friendly unit with an electric actuator to raise and lower the plows. These kind of plows often come equipped with very sharp and narrow knives that are spread evenly across the width of the frame.

Pulled behind a super-strong Bombardier Traxter, these knives break up root-filled and weedy soil well. But you'll have to make a few more passes with these to get the ground torn up enough for a disc. With only three knives, a lightweight chisel plow, such as the Weekend Warrior, tends to fall into the paths it has already cut, making it difficult to get in the areas in between those trenches.

A Weekend Warrior chisel plow has a convenient and simple hitch pin, which is connected to the quad's trailer hitch, but its short trailing arm sometimes causes the plow to jack knife quickly when backing up. You wouldn't get that with a frame-mounted three-point hitch-type plow unit, but with that setup you don't get the ease of hookup, either.

## Disc Time

Wiring the disc to the Weekend Warrior chisel plow is simple, though you may experience some electrical problems, such as blowing fuses. If this happens repeatedly, you can remove the fuse protection and wire it directly to the quad's battery. Once the disc is connected to the quad's trailer hitch, plug the wire connector together. This joins the battery power and electrical switch to the two actuators that raise and lower the disc.

Finally before discing dirt, you need to set the height of the disc. The disc can be raised for transport to the plowing site by moving a hitch pin on the trailering connection. Then you can lower the disc when you're ready to use it in the soil.

The Weekend Warrior disc can turn an overgrown grassy area into a well-groomed trail.

Thanks to the Bombardier Traxter and Weekend Warrior, you can turn the green earth into a deep shade of brown.

## Dirty Work

When digging in, you'll find that the two-row disc on the Weekend Warrior plow—with 10-inch diameter discs—works extremely well through the "cleaner" sections of earth, but it struggles significantly with sections of grassy dirt. If you add a good amount of weight to the rear end of the disc (100 pounds, for example), you can keep the disc from bouncing off the grassy clumps. But steadying a 100-pound weight on the frame is tricky.

On a newer Weekend Warrior plow, 12-inch discs add weight and break up deeper soil better.

The Weekend Warrior has a relatively simple construction, with actuators mounted over each of the two wheels to raise and lower the disc frame. These actuators are normally very durable; but you should check the mounting hardware and wiring connections frequently, especially if the unit is left outdoors, as is often the case.

Though the unit looks pretty large, it is easy to move around—even on a narrow plot of land. The length of the disc makes it easy to back up the unit. And since it's the same width as the ATV, you can gauge the disc's path without having to look behind you all the time. The Weekend Warrior is small enough to handle a large home garden or a small plot used for farming or hunting

| PROJECT 6 | Plowing Snow |
| --- | --- |

By Chaz Rice

**Time:** As long as it takes to get the job done

**Tools:** Socket set, boxend wrenches, screwdrivers, hammer, pliers

**Talent:** ★★

**Tab:** $200–$300

**Parts:** Plow blade, mounting system, lift system

**Tip:** Choose the right blade style for your needs

**Benefit:** Pushing snow is a lot easier with an ATV

**Complementary Project:** Adding heated grips and a cab enclosure

If you're not mowing grass, you're plowing snow, right? That's the way it always seems to go, even if you live in a place that allegedly has four seasons. So what can you do when the earth is blanketed with the white stuff? If you have a snow plow–equipped ATV, the answer is simple: Move it. But how does one decide which setup is the best among all the plows and accessories available for ATVs? This overview of plows and parts should help you narrow down your choices.

### Plows

This can be the most complicated part of the decision process. Not only do plows come in different shapes and sizes, they now come in different materials and colors.

A snow plow–equipped ATV in action.

The traditional option is a steel plow. Steel plows were the first on the market and are the most readily available option from aftermarket companies. Every company manufacturing plows today makes a steel plow for ATVs. These plows are constructed from heavy-gauge steel, usually around 11 gauge, and have replaceable wear bars or pads on the bottom edge of the plow.

The other option for blade material is plastic. Cycle Country offers this alternative with its Lite Force Plow blade. The blade is made from an eighth of an inch of high-density polyethylene. The advantage of a plastic blade is reduced weight; those at Cycle Country say a 60-inch plastic blade weighs about as much as a 48-inch steel blade.

## Width

After choosing the blade material, the next step is choosing how wide of a path to plow. Here a number of factors come into play. The first is what the blade will be used for. If you live in the suburbs or city and only plan to plow your driveway, a blade less than 50 inches wide may be the best option.

Narrower blades are lighter than wider blades, so they add less weight to the front of your machine. Secondly, a shorter blade helps in storing the ATV when it is not in use. For instance, if you use a shed to store your ATV, a 60-inch blade may not allow you to use that space unless the plow is removed.

For those in rural areas, a blade less than 48 inches wide may cause you and your quad to do more work in large plowing areas; the smaller the blade, the more time spent plowing the area. While larger blades are heavier, they can move much more snow at one time. You will, however, need a large machine to move a larger amount of snow. Most manufacturers recommend a quad engine that is 500 cc or larger for use with blades wider than 50 inches. Almost any ATV can handle a blade less than 50 inches, but a plow blade wider than that requires increased engine size.

One of the longest blades on the market is a 72-inch blade. It is recommended for utility vehicles such as Polaris' Ranger, Kawasaki's Mule, Yamaha's Rhino, and John Deere's Gator line.

## Shape

Believe it or not, you should consider different shapes of plow blades too. These include the traditional concave straight blades, but manufacturers have designed new configurations and styles in recent years.

Moose makes County Plow. This blade is shaped much like a blade found on the large plow trucks that

you see on county and city streets. The blade tapers from 26 inches on one end to 16 inches on the other end. This design aims to funnel snow to the side when you are plowing at higher speeds. In addition, the blade has a rubber flap at the top of it to prevent snow from flying into the face of the rider. Cycle Country also has a tapered blade called the State Blade.

Cycle Country's Power Vee blade is hinged at the middle to adjust to 16 different positions. A spring-loaded pin on the plow allows for the adjustment. The advantage of this plow, according to Cycle Country, is that you can select from numerous widths for plowing different-sized surfaces.

Depending on the material, shape, and width of the plow, costs will vary. Expect, however, to see prices starting at $130.

## Mounting Kits

With the blade chosen, the next step is figuring out how to attach it to the ATV. Most blades attach using push tubes. The push tube mounting plate attaches to the underside of the ATV somewhere near the middle of the ATV's frame. Most use the same mounting points as the ATV's skid plate, and they supply longer bolts to hold both the tube plate and the skid plate onto the ATV. While the push tubes are universal, the mounting brackets are machine-specific.

Here the plow's push tubes are on the left between the tires, and the blade (wear pads are the silver discs) is on the right.

Each company has a matrix of part numbers from which to choose your machine's mounting kit. These kits are made to be specific for different bolt patterns of the underside of the ATV. Make sure you know the year and make of your ATV before ordering the mounting kit. Push tube prices start around $100, and mounting kits retail for $60 or more.

The tubes then mount to the underside of the ATV via quick-release pins. The plow blade mounts to the push tubes and the tubes extend back from the blade. To mount the blade, all you have to do is drive over the push tubes and then reach under the ATV and line up the holes for the mounting pins.

Some manufacturers make quick-mount kits to simplify the plow-mounting process. Polaris, for instance, has its new Glacier Plow, which mounts to an ATV's frame and has a quick-release feature. The carrier stays connected to the ATV, even when the plow blade isn't attached. When you want to hook up the plow, you simply drive the ATV over the mounting hook and a V-shaped receiver engages the tongue. Then you can attach the winch and raise the blade to fully engage the connection. Removal is also simple. Lower the plow to the ground, disconnect the winch, and pull the pin; then back up the ATV to remove the plow from the machine.

Swisher also makes a universal mounting system that can attach a plow to an ATV. The plow bolts into a receiver on the front of the mounting system. The mounting system runs the length of the ATV's under-belly to distribute weight. The blade for the Swisher system is 50 inches wide.

Plow actuators are simply small winches that have enough power to raise and lower plows.

Winch controls mounted to the handlebars are convenient, but can be difficult to use when wearing bulky gloves.

### Lift Systems

Now that the plow is mounted to the machine, you may think you can go and move snow. Think again. The last part of the plowing puzzle is the lift system. A lift system raises the blade safely out of the way when riding the ATV. Here a buyer has three options.

For the svelte and muscular, there is the manual lift kit. This is the cheapest option; most start at about $100. Don't get the wrong idea, though. Plows aren't too heavy and don't require much effort to lift, but it is the repetitive action that makes people shy away from manual lift kits.

Manual lift kits consist of a handle that mounts to the front of the machine and runs beside the ATV operator. The operator pulls the handle back and the plow "clicks" out of the locked position and down into the plow position. When the rider wants to lift the blade, the handle is pulled back and "clicked" into the locked and lifted position.

If your ATV already has a winch mounted to the front of it, all plow manufacturers offer a winch lift option. These kits start around $100, but when you factor in the cost of the winch, they are much more expensive than the manual lift. These kits mount to the existing winch and the user operates the winch normally, but in smaller increments, to raise and lower the blade to the desired height.

With the winch kit, however, the ATV owner must be careful not to tax the winch by pulling on the blade after it reaches its maximum height. This can lead to premature wear and may snap the cable of the winch.

Also, do not allow too much slack in the cable when plowing. This can kink the cable inside the winch and weaken the cable.

The last lift option is the electric lift kit or plow actuator. This is much like a winch lift kit, but it is for those who want the convenience of a winch lift, but do not want to invest in a winch.

The kit consists of a "mini winch" that mounts to the push tube. The electric lift kit has a handlebar-mounted control and is attached to the ATV's battery. The winches are sealed from the elements and are heavy-duty enough to lift any plow blade. These kits usually have a pulley that mounts on the front rack of the ATV to lift the blade and feature a "quick-release" cable for when the plow blade is not in use. Electric lift kits start at $150.

### Accessories

There are a ton of accessories for plows, from replaceable wear bars to plow blade skids that mount to the bottom of the plow and allow the user to adjust the plow height. Most companies also offer side shields that mount on the edges of the plow. These shields reduce the amount of snow "overflowing" from the sides of the blade.

Plow users may need to consider buying tire chains. Traction is reduced on snow and ice, and using chains may increase traction greatly. But chains can also dig into driveways and slash brake lines if installed improperly or on the wrong machine. Strapping sandbags to the ATV racks is another easy way to increase traction.

<table>
<tr><td>**PROJECT 7**</td><td># Adding Heated Grips</td></tr>
</table>

By Glenn Hansen

**Time:** 45 minutes

**Tools:** Screwdrivers, utility knife, wire stripper, metric socket set

**Talent:** ★★

**Tab:** $50

**Parts:** Heated grip kit

**Tip:** Mount switch to be easily visible so you don't leave the grip's power on and drain the ATV's battery

**Benefit:** Warm hands on cold riding days

You don't need a Minnesota winter to appreciate the wonder of heated grips. They might not be necessity outside of the frozen great north, but they are a great convenience. They also make you a much happier ATV rider on cold days when your fingers would otherwise feel like popsicles when you got home.

Snowmobilers have long enjoyed warm hands while they ride in the cold because heated grips are standard equipment on many sleds. Now ATVers can have the same luxury with hot grips, allowing them to ride with those sledders in the coldest of weather.

Hot grips come in a variety of colors. Their high/low switch mounts best just below the bars of your ATV.
*Lee Klancher*

## Installation

Heated grips are easy to use, but not easy to install. First, you should plan ahead so you're not installing the grips when it's cold outside; otherwise, you'll freeze your hands trying to install handwarmers—the irony.

Most hot grips kits include everything you need for installation—the grips, some wire, a resistor, and a switch. You will need higher-than-average wiring skills to get these all working properly. You'll also need to solder a few connections and make sense of a rough wiring diagram.

The grips themselves go on fairly easily, but you'll need some good glue and might need to use a good file to get them to fit. After getting them on, you'll need to use your wire cutters and stripper, your solder, and the shrink-wrap connectors. Follow the directions closely, and call the product helpline if you get stuck in the process.

A closeup of the controls of a Grip Heater unit that has been installed on a Honda Rubicon.

## Turn up the Heat

If you flick the switch on but get no heat, you probably have a bad ground connection. On the Honda we were adding hot grips to, the proper ground connection was on the engine.

Once installed and wired correctly, the hot grips do take awhile to warm up, but when they get warmed up, you won't be thinking about the wait anymore—or how much time it took to install them. Both high and low heat options are available on these grips. The lower setting would be great to use while out riding on a cool spring or fall day. In harsh winter temperatures, you'll want to stick with the high setting and also keep a good pair of gloves on while out on a ride or plowing a lot of snow.

With plowing, you probably won't have much of a problem with wind, but temperatures will probably be colder as you most likely will plow early in the morning or in the evening. For the higher speeds of trail riding, cold winds will compound the cold temperatures. If you're an avid winter rider, you may want to add an extra wind break to your quad, such as a big windshield or at least some hand guards.

The only shortcoming of the hot grips (besides the time-consuming wiring need to install them) is that they're slippery. Their slickness probably won't cause much of a problem if you're slow-speed plowing and firewood gathering, but for a trail ride, this slickness could cause you to loose your grip.

<table>
<tr><td>**PROJECT 8**</td><td># Loading & Transporting ATVs</td></tr>
</table>

By Chaz Rice

**Time:** 1 to 2 hours

**Tools:** Minimal tools

**Talent:** ★★

**Tab:** $100–$800

**Parts:** Some sort of loading system

**Benefit:** Simplifying the ATV-loading process

**Complementary Project:** Truck or trailer maintenance

Getting ready for your next weekend ATV ride can be a real chore, especially when it comes to loading your quad in an out of a truck bed. For those of us who just love to be out on the trail every Saturday, finding an easy way to load and transport our ATVs becomes as essential as picking the next weekend's adventure.

## Load Pro

For those looking for a very simple solution, look no further than the Load Pro. The Load Pro is a gift from the gods because of how easy it makes loading and transporting ATVs.

If you had a Load Pro, you would soon learn to hate ramps, especially after completing a tiring race. The last thing anyone wants to do after racing in the woods two-plus hours on an ATV is lug around some heavy ATV ramps. Or maybe it has been a long day on the job and the last thing you want to do is dig the ramps out of the truck bed.

Remember the last time you were tired and had to unload the ramps—yep, you slipped and scratched your new truck. Without those ramps, your rig wouldn't have that scratch. Again, eliminate them.

The Load Pro comes in two sizes—one for a short bed and one for regular beds. The key to the Load Pro is

Here is the Load Pro stored in the reinforced steel deck. This gives you full use of the truck bed.

its raised deck. This deck neatly fits the footprint of your truck's bed and conceals the loading ramp when not in use. This deck is four inches higher than the truck bed, is made from reinforced steel, and can carry the same load as a normal truck bed. It is also powder-coated and sprayed with a truck bed liner.

To load an ATV, simply open the tailgate and pull the large ramp from under this deck and voilà, there is your ramp. The ramp rolls in and out from the deck easily. The Load Pro also comes with two rubber inserts that provide a smooth transition from the ramp to the deck. These help quite a bit as wheels can get hung up on the four-inch rise of the deck. These inserts can then store behind the wheel wells and out of the way.

Once fully extended, just drive your ATV up and into the bed of the truck.

Rubber tailgate inserts aid in loading an ATV into the truck.

The loading ramp is nicely constructed from steel and has a perforated surface for traction. It also allows dirt and snow to fall through. The zinc-plated ramp can hold up to 1,500 pounds. The ramp even features a large rubber handle that is easy to grab.

The Load Pro mounts in the back of the truck bed with two brackets that bolt to the vertical panel between the tailgate and box. All you need to do to mount the Load Pro is drill two holes for the brackets. That's it.

The short bed version ($699) is 74 inches long and the regular bed version ($799) is 92.5 inches long. Yes, way more money than ramps. Both are 48 inches wide so they fit between the wheel wells and can accommodate most utility ATVs. Total weight of the short bed version is 265 pounds, while the regular bed version is 330 pounds. The Load Pro is available for most full-size trucks from Ford, GM, Dodge, and Toyota.

## TK Loader

In the world of ATV loading ramps, the TK Loader is the 42-inch, flat-screen, high-definition plasma wall-mount television with picture-in-picture and nine-watt-per-channel stereo amplifier. Of course, a lot of guys just like regular old ramps too.

The TK Loader is a unique tool for loading an ATV, snowmobile, lawn tractor, or other equipment. Three electric Superwinch winches are connected to steel and plastic platforms, and the whole 340-pound assemblage mounts in the bed of a pickup truck. Wired to a 12-volt supply—either a separate battery or your truck's electric—a remote operator maneuvers the platform to retrieve the goods.

**Above and next page:** Is it too much? Only if you like to do absolutely everything yourself. For heavy ATVs like this big 4x4, the TK Loader is the king of convenience.

We mounted the TK Loader into the short box of our Chevy Silverado. However, we were unable to close the tailgate. In order to retain full use of the truck bed, you should load the TK Loader in a truck with a full-size bed.

It works like this: To load an ATV onto the TK Loader, the user-activated chain-driven motor slides the platform out the back of the truck; then the platform tilts, ramp-like, to load the machine. The winch cable then runs out to the ATV, and the process is reversed. It's a sweatless and mostly brainless one-person operation.

The unit is incredibly easy to use; anyone who can read and operate a toggle switch can control the winches and the TK Loader's movements. The unit's electrical supply is controlled by a key for safety.

Another advantage is that you can load machines as heavy as the Polaris Sportsman 700, close to 800 pounds, as easily as a lightweight sport quad. The TK Loader is rated to load 1,000 pounds. When you use this loader in the winter, you should keep the hand-operated control covered to keep it from freezing. Otherwise, you'll have to find a way to warm it enough to get it working again.

The manufacturer also has several add-ons available to make the TK Loader more versatile, turning it into a small dump cart or a motorcycle hauler, for example.

**Travel Master Loading System**

This loading system and rack allows space for two ATVs in a long-bed, full-size truck, thus giving you the option of going without a trailer on a day-long jaunt.

The loading system and rack are made of small-diameter square tubing, which looks much the same as wrought iron, and are easy to assemble (despite the fact they comes in a lot of separate boxes). The first step is to attach the system's two main rails to each side of the truck's bed rails. Then bolt the cross ramps to these. This is probably the only part of the assembly that requires much thought, as the Travel Master allows adjustment in widths for different-sized ATVs.

The Travel Master has tubular side rails to help guide the ATV up and down the ramps.

Because the tow vehicle's hitch is left free, you have room to pull a camper or trailer.

The long ramps used to load the ATVs on the truck need only to have the two halves connected with the hinge bolt. So in the end, you can get the rack and ramps put together in less than an hour. It's that easy!

### Loading Hazards?

The first question that anyone has upon seeing the Travel Master is, "How scary is it loading?" The first thing you should know about this is that the ramps of the system slide into a truck's lip, which holds them in place while loading. They also each have a tubular side rail on the outside that keeps an ATV's tires on the

ramp during the trip up or down. Lastly, the system included a safety rail that keeps the ATV from over-driving the truck bed—adding greatly to the confidence while loading.

Now to really answer that question . . . After loading several different two-wheel drive utility machines during testing, we only had a few problems with wheel slippage while trying to back up and over the arch to get off the truck. Loading Honda 400EXs and modified Banshees also proved easy to load, but did pose some challenges. First, the sport quads with low-profile tires bottomed out on the side rails. Second, unloading an

ATV without reverse proved somewhat more of a challenge than we had anticipated. The ATV has to be pushed up over the arch, yet not be allowed to escape and roll down the ramp.

The cross ramps on the truck are arched to provide more loading space in the truck bed. This arch also helps to lock the ATV in place once on the truck.

Another item to note: The Travel Master can be lifted off of the truck by two people in just a couple of minutes or disassembled and removed in less than 15 minutes.

### Transport, Tie-Down Options

Tie-downs are as valuable to an ATV enthusiast as duct tape is to any MacGyver wannabe. They are just so darn versatile—perfect for securing a quad, holding a loading ramp in place, or acting as an emergency tow rope.

Eventually, though, tie-downs can get rusty, rot, rip, and more—depending on how you take care of them. Recently, the ATV market has exploded with different products, including those that help secure your quad while in transport so you don't have to replace those tie-downs. Some of these products include the Trailer Vise, the Hasty Hitch, and the ATV Lock & Hold-Down.

### *Trailer Vise*

Outdoor Innovations' Trailer Vise isn't the smallest piece of trailer equipment you'll ever see, but it does work effectively. And the installation process is easy.

Having a drill is a must for installing all the trailer kits that keep ATVs secure during transport.

The Trailer Vise essentially hugs the ATV's tires, keeping it safe and secure.

Once you've measured the width of your ATV (from the center of each front tire) and figured the exact location where you want the vise to go, it's time to install the unit. You want to use the backing plate (provided) as your drilling template. After drilling the four installation holes, set up the two securing arms, with the side bars and chains pre-assembled, by sticking the two 3/8-inch bolts through each piece and through the trailer's floor. (You may need to purchase longer bolts to ensure a proper fit.)

Now, you'll need to crawl underneath the trailer to mount the backing plate, washers, and nuts (all provided).

Once you're finished installing the Trailer Vise, you're set for the easiest part— securing an ATV. This requires that you drive the quad onto the trailer until the front tires touch the vertical support beams. Next, simply spread the two chains around the back of the tires until the lateral side bars "squeeze" the tire firmly. Finally, you must decide where to place the master chain link. You need to get the master link to fit inside the lever lock. After closing the lever lock, you can add a padlock for extra security.

On a trail ride, the vise holds strong. It's also versatile enough that you can back your ATV on the trailer. You may need to move the master link up to fit the larger rear tires, but it still fits securely.

### *The Hasty Hitch*

It will take only a matter of minutes to drill the holes for this hitch in your trailer's plywood floor. But you'll probably need to change the size of your drill bit so you avoid making contact with the backing plate—the device used as a guide for installation.

Once the holes are drilled, you need to insert the four supplied bolts (3/8 x 1 1/2 inch) into the base plate assembly. (Make sure the holes for the lynch pin are facing the rear of the trailer.) From that point, you may need a little help, depending on the size of your trailer and the installation point you selected. The next step requires you to lie underneath the rear of the trailer and hold the backing plate up to the four protruding bolts. Then, add the four lock washers and nuts to the bolts, and crank them down.

Next you must slide the 90-degree tube through the base plate assembly. Then, slide the lynch pin into the hole closest to the 90-degree tube and through the hole nearest the end of the base plate assembly.

Now, slide the head assembly on to the 90-degree tube and tighten it using the locking knob. An end cap and drive screw also must be added to the 90-degree tube.

This installation can be nerve-racking at times. It may not easily fit with your ATV's hitch. It does keep your ATV secure during transport, though, once you get it configured. Yet you still may want to use a tie-down on the front of the ATV to prevent the front suspension from bouncing while being transported.

### ATV Lock & Hold-Down

This trailer add-on is one of the coolest and swiftest ones around. To install the Fulton device, you need to drill four 3/8-inch holes, for the 5/16-inch bolts, in the trailer's floor. Next, drill two additional 1/2-inch holes for the 3/8-inch U-bolt.

Now, place the mounting plates over the holes and insert the four corner bolts through the top bracket. Slide the U-bolt through its designated holes to check whether it moves freely. Next, attach the underside mounting plate. Tighten the corners of the mounting plate, checking to see if the U-bolt still slides freely.

Now, slide the U-bolt through both mounting plates and attach the locking device to the underside. Adjust the nuts, U-bolt, and locking device to allow an 1/8-inch clearance for the lock hook to fit into. The locking nuts are designed to fit inside the locking device when the U-bolt is pulled upward.

Next, load your quad and attach the larger lock hook to the ATV's axle. Attach the smaller, exposed metal hook to the U-bolt. Before locking the device, compress the quad's suspension, then ratchet it closed.

This whole installation and operation sounds more difficult than it really is.

Utilizing the quad's trailer hitch, the Hasty Hitch acts as an anti-theft device, as well as a bolt-on tie-down.

With the soft tie strap, this Powertye tie-down is kind to your ATV and is still secure.

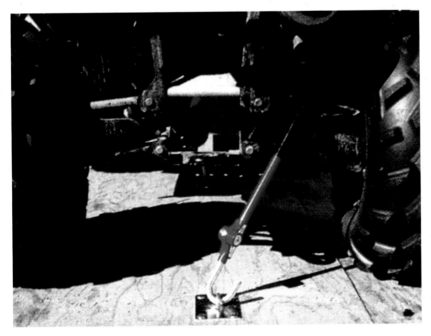

Fulton's ATV Lock & Hold-Down uses a ratchet-type system and can be used on a trailer or in a truck bed.

# PROJECT 9 | Selecting the Right Transport Trailer

Staff Report

**Time:** As long as it takes to find the right one for you

**Tools:** Your brain

**Talent:** ★★

**Tab:** $400–$15,000-plus

**Tip:** Take your time to find the best deal

**Benefit:** A good trailer means a good trip

There are a lot of trailers to haul ATVs in this world. The good news is that there are multiple trailers that suit your needs. The bad news is you'll have to sift through a lot of trailers to find the right one. How do you choose?

Take inventory of everything you need to haul: ATVs, riding lawn mowers, dirt bikes, construction equipment, and even your family. No matter what combination of goods you have to transport, there's a trailer ready for the task.

### Open or Shut Case

Let's start with the basics: Trailers for ATVs can be enclosed or open. Enclosed trailers are like portable garages, complete with walls and a roof. They are great at hauling ATVs for long distances and they protect quads. Cargo inside stays dry and the trailers can tote other items, such as gas cans, gear, and attachments. Enclosed trailers range in size. The small ones fit one ATV and the massive units boast enough space to lug four or five quads behind a tow vehicle. Before you haul all the quads in your neighborhood, though, be sure your vehicle is rated to tow the weight loaded into the enclosed trailer.

Open trailers are flat beds without roofs and walls. Some have side rails around the edges to protect the cargo. Others are simply a flat carrying area with tie-down mounts bolted into the bed.

There are advantages and disadvantages of both designs. The biggest advantage of an enclosed trailer is that it can haul more stuff and haul it more securely. It creates a shelter from wind or rain, can be heated and, while you're sleeping, is a secure location to keep ATVs. The walls of the enclosed trailer can hold cabinets and shelves to create organized storage spaces.

The disadvantages of enclosed trailers include that they are heavier than open trailers, they can catch the wind, and therefore the tow vehicle consumes more fuel.

Pace American, AeroSport

TPD's composite trailer is an enclosed unit constructed with a one-piece fiberglass-reinforced panel. These trailers are special-order items in which the customer can select the desired features. Pace American also makes enclosed trailers. The AeroSport offers plenty of standard features plus a ton of options. AeroSport models are available in 6-, 7-, and 8.5-foot widths; 11- to 36-foot lengths; and in single-, tandem-, and triple-axle configurations.

Fifth-wheel trailers are a subcategory of enclosed trailers. They do not hook up to a conventional hitch at the rear of a vehicle, but instead secure to a mount in the bed of a pickup truck. The advantage of a fifth-wheel trailer is better weight distribution to the tow vehicle and a more spacious interior.

Since the "hitch" resides in the bed of the pickup truck, the load is directly above the rear wheels. This location improves traction and makes pulling a large trailer much easier. As for making the interior more spacious, a fifth-wheel trailer allows for separate storage quarters above the truck's bed inside the trailer.

Drawbacks to this style of trailer are they're more expensive than traditional hitch trailers and you must have a truck capable of towing a fifth-wheel trailer.

As explained above, one of the biggest advantages of an open trailer is its weight. These trailers weigh next to nothing—especially the aluminum ones—yet can carry a lot of ATVs. But there isn't built-in shelter or storage. If you haul an ATV in the northern states during winter, you'll have to use an ATV cover or wash the road spray off the ATV because an ATV's metal parts can oxidize due to salt put on the roads.

Another advantage of the open trailer is its price. An open trailer is much cheaper than an enclosed design. Also, some open trailers can do double duty. The BK1000U from ShoreLand'r is an open trailer that can haul an ATV and be towed by an ATV.

### Hauling by Numbers

Do you have one ATV? Two ATVs? An entire fleet of ATVs? Single-place trailers are perfect for casual recreationists who only need to haul one machine and minimal cargo. Two-place trailers are great for double ATV duty, or for a single ATV and a load of gear. If you have a half-dozen quads to tote, there are trailers for that too.

Buying a single-place trailer might suit your needs now, but think before you plunk down cash for one. Do you foresee any needs in the future for more hauling capacity? A single-place trailer has very specific limits: one ATV. A two-place trailer can just as easily haul one ATV and give you room to expand your fleet.

### Beaver Tail

Beaver-tail trailers have a hinged, single fold-down ramp for loading. Enclosed trailers feature a beaver tail that doubles as the rear door of the trailer. Open trailers can also sport a beaver tail that is slatted metal and doubles as a single ramp for loading the ATV and then folds up.

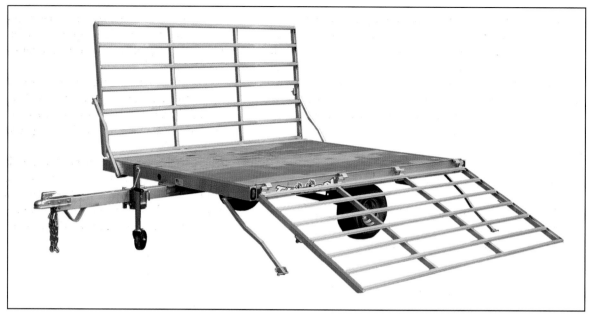

Triton, SL8

Triton offers a number of trailers, including beaver-tail styles. The SL8 is a side-loading model made of aluminum with a half-inch, marine-grade plywood bed. It offers quick-release pins on the 46-inch-high extruded ramps and a four-cord rubber torsion axle.

## Ramp Style

Ramp-style trailers can mimic the beaver tails' fold-down action, but they do it with twice the fold-downs. This trailer has permanent, built-in ramps, so unloading is never an issue and lugging a bulky set of ramps along for the ride isn't necessary.

Featherlite's 1694 model is aluminum and features two sizes of ramps that can double as side rails. The ramps can be attached to the rear and both sides (ahead and behind the fender) for either side or rear loading. With two ramp sizes, this model makes loading an ATV painless. It's available in lengths of 10 and 12 feet. It also features eight rubber-coated tie-down rings.

ShoreLand'r, BK2ATV

Featherlite, 1694

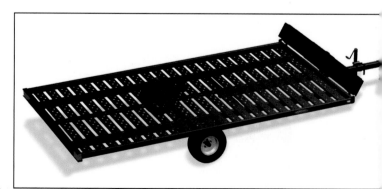

ShoreLand'r, BK3ATV

ShoreLand'r also manufactures ramp-style trailers. The BK2ATV and the BK3ATV have steel tube frames with a powder-coat finish. The models feature steel platform decks with holes to provide traction and aid in cleanup. Two removable ramps are stored at the front of the trailer to shield ATVs from road debris. The ramps can be positioned almost anywhere around the trailer frame for loading.

### 'Toybox'

Think of toybox trailers as a house and garage on wheels. The front portion of the trailer has living quarters, complete with a couch and kitchenette, and the rear part is a garage and sleeping area.

ThorCalifornia offers two toybox trailers: the Fury Tahoe and the Vortex. ThorCalifornia offers these trailers in varying lengths. Optional amenity packages can tailor the trailer to your needs.

They have laminated aluminum-frame sidewalls and fiberglass exteriors. The cargo floor is made of seamless StructurWood with tie-downs anchored into the steel chassis of the trailer. These trailers are prime for a recreational family.

A company that is new to the "toybox" market is Fleetwood RV. Its line of GearBOX LSV trailers are designed for motorsports enthusiasts. These trailers offer features such as onboard air compressors and fuel tanks and pumps, which are ideal for ATVs. Also, the

ThorCalifornia, Fury Tahoe

ThorCalifornia, Vortex

interior options for the GearBOX line include a motor-sports theme—complete with diamond plate and a dark gray color that makes any garage rat feel at home.

## Wheeless Trailers

Lots of parts, pieces, and hardware—that's what the Mesa Verde Quad Rack Trailer is all about. These extras make this wheeless trailer very usable.

Once assembled, you can tilt the rack for loading simply by pulling the release pin on the tilt latch and releasing the locking "slam latch." If your pickup truck is a taller one, you'll instantly appreciate the extension ramp that comes with the trailer and makes loading and unloading an ATV or other wheeled equipment much easier. The slam latch lock feature grabs the ramp bed once you've loaded the quad and dropped it back to level—making loading a quad onto the Mesa Verde a one-person operation, if it works as designed. When tested, the slam latch didn't work every time, though.

The ramp extension makes loading the Mesa Verde rack quite easy.

When the rack is not loaded with toys, the tilt feature is great.

If you're loading a rear-end heavy ATV, or another piece of equipment that is stern heavy, you can extend the front of the Mesa Verde rack to ease tilting it back to the flat driving position. In this extended position, the Quad Rack is 80 inches long. This rack is rated to carry 700 pounds, and the manufacturer says it has tested it with more than 1,000 pounds loaded. The rack itself weighs 190 pounds.

The other feature that's great on this trailer is its three-position locking tilt mechanism, which includes a normal driving position, a slightly raised position for driving your rack-loaded truck through really rough terrain, and a raised-and-out-of-the-way position for city driving, parking, and unloaded use. This feature is available in the deluxe package.

The Mesa Verde rack requires some assembly. It is a simple process, but it does require the work of two guys take two people to lift and hold the heavy pieces. Also you'll need to do the taillight wiring during the assembly process.

If your Mesa Verde rack spends most of its time outside, it will pick up some rust, but it will still work well as a utility tool.

The Carry-All Rack is a simpler utility tool. It has no fancy features, just a tilt bed and a short side rail. Yet it's not as easy to use as the Mesa Verde rack.

To tilt the Carry-All Rack, remove the large bolt that screws in place to lock the rack down. Carry-All provides a "wrench" of sorts that is kept with the rack for when it's time to tilt it or lock it in place. This wrench is essentially a piece of steel with a hex-head opening cut into the bottom to grab the bolt.

This Kawasaki Prairie fits on the Carry-All Rack, though it's best to "walk" ATVs on to the ramp.

There is a grease fitting at the rack's pivot point to help keep the unit's essential part in working condition. The rack comes with four small steel caster wheels on one end. You can stand the rack on end and move it around your garage for easy storage.

The Carry-All is wired and ready to go when you receive it. And like the Mesa Verde, it is a heavy steel unit, but it can be mounted to a truck's receiver hitch by one person. It will take two people to get an ATV loaded safely onto the rack, however.

For use on some trucks, the Carry-All could use a ramp extension. If your truck is pretty tall, the Carry-All's short rack bed becomes a pretty steep ramp when hooked to a tall receiver hitch.

The Carry-All is rated to hold 600 pounds. The manufacturer has tested it with more weight, but doesn't recommend hauling more, mainly because of trailer hitch limitations. The rack itself weighs about 170 pounds.

The Carry-All Rack is a good option because of its simple design. Little is likely to break on this rack, and if it did, you could easily fix it. But the Mesa Verde rack does have more easy-to-use features and a more user-friendly design.

<table>
<tr><td>## PROJECT 10</td><td># Buying a Trailer or Rack Box</td></tr>
</table>

Staff Report

**Time:** Again, as long as you want to keep at it

**Tools:** Your brain

**Talent:** ★★

**Tab:** $100–$15,000-plus

**Tip:** Pay close attention to quality

**Benefit:** Pick the right one and your ATV life will be much easier

Whether you are farming, ranching, landscaping, or just hauling a lot of stuff around, you're probably in need of a solid utility trailer or rack box—especially one that can carry supplies for a variety of tasks. Finding one that is so versatile can be tough, though. The choices abound, and finding differences between them is sometimes a challenge.

### Husky Hauler Trailer

One company that offers a lot of quality "jack-of all-trades" trailers and rack boxes is Nordell. The manufacturer's most popular line is its Husky Haulers. The trailer in this line is, according to Nordell, "high speed," as it can handle speeds above 10 miles per hour with a full load. For this trailer, a full load is 1,500 pounds. And the 18-inch flotation tires let the Husky trailer roll smoothly over any terrain—from plowed fields to rough woods.

The relatively small and lightweight unit connects to a trailer hitch with a bolt or hitch pin. The trailer's short tongue keeps it close to the machine for easy handling around tight corners, and it's still simple to back up.

This Husky duo from Nordell Manufacturing will help with any job around the farm.

The trailer can also be used as a dump box by pulling a pin on the trailer's frame. The big plastic box tilts easily for dumping a load of sand or rock, and it is easily locked back into place.

After months of use in a range of harsh conditions—summer heat to winter chill, dirt roads to rough fields—this trailer works flawlessly. It even works well and looks good after being heavily abused. In fact, this trailer's resilience is almost hard to believe.

### Husky Hauler Sportsmen

This rack box in the Husky Hauler line is a deep, two-compartment plastic box that connects with U-bolts to any tubular rear rack. The smaller compartment is designed to carry a gun or bow. Specially designed foam inserts are included to help anchor these valuables. Then the lid can be held shut with a padlock for extra security. The larger front compartment will hold almost anything.

Measuring 43 inches across, the box is almost as wide as an ATV. The 16-inch depth gives you lots of room for big loads of tools or other goods.

The Husky Hauler is made of quarter-inch thick "UV-stabilized polyethylene" and is roto-molded to keep it watertight, according to the manufacturer. It uses two U-bolts as anchors, and these keep the box secure, even when the quad is being driven through rough woods trails. Plus, with the use of just two U-bolts, you can easily remove the box.

Normally, rack boxes might not take the kind of abuse given to a utility trailer, but because Nordell products are known for their durability, this one probably can take quite a beating.

### Cycle Country Fifth-Wheel Trailer

The term "fifth wheel" usually describes giant trailers used to haul everything from race quads to horses. Cycle Country's version of a fifth-wheel trailer also hauls a wide variety of items—just on a smaller scale.

This handy box will work on the farm or on the hunt with its locking gun holder.

The Cycle Country fifth-wheel trailer is one of the most versatile haulers on the market.

The hitch assembly of the trailer mounts to the assembly for a hitch ball on your ATV. The hitch is mildly complicated to assemble because the bolt that holds the hitch to the ATV has a two-inch head that requires a little digging to find something large enough to tighten it; a channel-lock pliers will do the trick.

The trailer comes with two five-inch inflatable tires that ride under the trailer's two main beams. When we first assembled the trailer, we had our doubts. The wheelbase of the trailer was awfully small at just more than two feet. On the trail, however, the small wheelbase of the trailer was a bonus. The trailer tracked extremely well when empty on a rough trail, complete with tight, twisty turns.

Any trailer can perform empty; the real test is when loaded. Hay bales—or was it straw?—were a perfect test. By using the trailer's built-in extension, we carried the bales easily.

The only drawback to this trailer is that the hitch doesn't rotate well when you're tracking through off-camber trails. This makes the trailer feel tippy when going in rough terrain.

Arguably the best feature of the Cycle Country trailer is its storage option. When the trailer is not in use and high-speed transport is needed, just mount the trailer on racks Cycle Country supplies with the kit. The racks mount to the ATV's rear racks with universal clamps.

## LMI Welding ATV Trailer

Filling a different niche in the ATV trailer world is LMI Welding's ATV trailer. This Montana-based manufacturer makes a top-notch trailer that can handle all types of abuse. The trailer assembles easily and is very well built.

The 48-inch width and large tires of the LMI ATV trailer help it track well, even in rough terrain.

A great feature of this trailer is its suspension system. The two suspension housings that come with the trailer are rated at 500 pounds each. When trailering heavy loads, you notice the difference the suspension makes, as trailer bounce is greatly reduced. Even when loaded with 450 pounds of sandbags, the trailer does not bounce.

The trailer kit also comes with two knobby tires on steel wheels that were impressive. LMI didn't cut any corners with the tires as they feature a tread similar to that of Titan's Turf Tamers. The trailer's basket is 48

How's this for utility hauling?

inches long, and the wheelbase of the trailer is as wide as most ATVs.

To accommodate even longer loads, the trailer box has removable front and rear gates. When removed, the gates mount out of the way on the side of the box. In addition, the trailer has an extendable tongue to accommodate longer loads, which made turning easier.

The trailer attaches to the ATV using a standard hitch with two-inch ball. On our rough woods course, the trailer tracked well when empty. The combination of the two suspension housings and the tires allowed the trailer to perform flawlessly when heavily loaded.

This trailer is a perfect fit for those who need to carry large, heavy loads through all types of terrain, particularly rough terrains. For transporting a harvested deer, this trailer would be ideal. The trailer retails for $695, plus shipping. It is available directly from LMI Welding.

### Equinox Industries Ox Cart

The Ox Cart is one of the tallest ATV trailers we've ever tested. The frame of the trailer is constructed from thick powder-coated steel tubing. The bed is made from a polyethylene plastic and comes in a variety of colors. A camo cover can be purchased separately.

Assembling the trailer is a breeze and requires a minimal amount of tools. The trailer attaches to the ATV using the traditional hitch and ball. The tongue of the hitch is a little short, but that doesn't affect the trailer's performance.

The wheels and tires of the trailer compare to those on the LMI Welding trailer in their size and style. The main difference is that the Ox Cart has a solid axle. In testing, the tires did a great job of tracking through our course when the trailer was both loaded and empty. For carrying capacity, Equinox says the Ox Cart can handle 1,500 pounds.

When it comes to comparing this trailer to others, it is apples to oranges. Even with the optional utility racks that increase the trailer's bed depth from 12 to 24 inches, the Ox Cart isn't really a "utility" trailer, but rather a "recreational" trailer. It would be the perfect trailer to load a tent, sleeping bags, food, etc., in order to pull behind your ATV for a weekend trip.

The bed was much too high to load anything of weight, like a load of dirt. Lowering would help, but that would compromise the trailer's axle setup and ground clearance. One advantage the Ox Cart has is its narrow wheelbase that allows it to fit into tighter spaces, and that makes this trailer more maneuverable.

The Equinox Ox Cart

# PROJECT 11 | Towing Trailers Safely

By Jerrod Kelley

**Time:** As long as it takes to get where you are going . . . safely

**Tools:** Tie-downs, spare trailer tire

**Talent:** ★★

**Parts:** A wiring harness that connects the tow vehicle's light wiring to the trailer, brake controls (optional)

**Tip:** Don't drive a tow vehicle with a trailer like a race car; use caution and plenty of common sense

**Benefit:** Getting the trailer to your destination safely, without harming individuals or your ATV

When it comes to trailering, we at *ATV Magazine* should be considered experts. We've toted ATVs all over the United States, and in a variety of ways, with several different types of hauling devices. Because of our first-hand experience, we've learned many trailering techniques that could save you from that potential mishap that's lingering around the next corner. Here are just a few of them.

Always expect the unexpected when trailering. Your potential laziness in preparation could hurt other drivers if something does go wrong.

Before you leave your driveway, inspect the safety hooks for wear.

## Mishaps & Lessons Learned

**Oops No. 1:** A blown-out tire on a rental RV-type trailer sent us on a four-hour treasure hunt to find a spare, on a Sunday no less.

*Lesson:* Always carry a spare tire, and the tools to change it.

**Oops No. 2:** When a trailer's safety hooks detached from the cable, the trailer nearly caused a major accident on the interstate.

*Lesson:* Check all your trailer's attachments, including cables, anchor hooks, and various devices. Some states require that all hooks must have a closure device on them. It's a good idea to have this type of hook, regardless of the law.

**Oops No. 3:** Once a Honda Foreman—in gear with the parking brake on in the back of our truck—crashed through our rear window, sending glass everywhere, after an abrupt stop. Luckily, everything turned out fine.

*Lesson:* Always tie down your ATV, no matter how you are hauling it. It's hard to hold back a 600-pound quad if you have to stop abruptly.

**Oops No. 4:** When a hitch ball bolt sheared off on the interstate, our trailer started darting from lane to lane.

*Lesson:* Always check to see if your trailer hitch bolt and nut is properly tightened. You should also have a spare hitch assembly in case something like this should happen.

**Oops No. 5:** While we were towing an empty trailer in very icy conditions, it fishtailed out of control. After all was said and done, damages included a bent trailer tongue, missing loading ramps, a broken trailer light, and various dents.

*Lesson:* Be cautious when towing an empty trailer, especially in unfavorable weather conditions. It's better to be safe than sorry. You won't have to repair your trailer if you avoid this situation.

Always look over your trailer's welds before you use it.

## Trailer Inspection

Before you even begin to load your ATVs, do a once-over on your trailer and tow vehicle. Check the wheels and tires and all the components on the trailer's tongue. Take a quick look at the trailer's welds. It would suck to lose your beaver tail on the interstate—and more so for the guy behind you! Next, inspect the floor of your trailer. Rotting wood or loose D-rings could be a major problem.

Once you're set to attach your trailer to your tow vehicle, inspect your anchor hooks, tongue-to-ball connection, and your electrical hookup. This is also the best time to examine your trailer and tow vehicle's lights. Non-working brake lights are obviously a bad thing.

Now you're set to load your ATV(s). The objective is to find an equal (level) placement for the ATV that lets the trailer sit level to the ground. Be sure to balance the weight over the axle if you're loading more than one quad. Also, if you plan on hauling other supplies—gas cans, ramps, rack boxes, etc.—on the trailer, remember, you can never have enough tie-downs.

## Tie 'Em Down

Double-check every tie-down you use. Toss out those partially torn straps or old units that you found on the trail. Spending $7 for a new one is cheaper than replacing the ATV that just bounced off your ride, or the ramp that just flew off and hit that car behind you.

Tie-downs are a necessity.

Ratchet tie-downs work best because they are easier to tighten. But manual tie-downs work well too, though they require a bit more muscle. Be cautious when strapping them to your ATV. If you want your plastic or tie-rod to remain in good condition, don't anchor the hook of the strap to them. Use the racks or a solid part of the chassis. Also, be sure to compress the quad's suspension. This will almost eliminate the suspension bouncing during transport, and it will secure your tie-downs.

## What Else Should You Do?

Once you've decided it's safe to enter traffic, you should travel at an adequate speed. Use good judgment and keep the weather and road conditions in mind. In fact, be ready for weather changes by watching the forecast—though you shouldn't necessarily trust that.

Depending on the size of your city, keep an eye on the traffic conditions too.

Another good idea—depending on how far you're traveling and what types of roads (gravel, paved, rough, etc.) you're on—is to stop and inspect the tie-downs, or anything else that may have come loose. Sometimes you have to remind yourself that you have a much longer tow vehicle now. You can't pass that slow driver as easily as before—use caution. You should also always carry tools (anything you may need), including a spare trailer tire, flares, and locks in case you have to abandon the trailer and ATV(s) when you go to get help.

From there, it's pretty much out of your hands. You sometimes just have to be patient and hope the trailering gods have decided to bless you on your journey. However, with advance planning and inspection, you can avoid almost any potential trailer problems.

# SECTION 2
# ON THE TRAIL

Projects 12-20

| PROJECT 12 | Riding Safely |
|---|---|

By John Woods

**Time:** As long as you ride, any time you ride

**Tools:** Safety gear, including a helmet, long-sleeve shirt, gloves, goggles, and boots

**Talent:** ★★

**Parts:** Protective riding gear

**Tip:** Ride according to your ability; don't push past sensible limits

**Benefit:** Unbroken bones and a healthy ATV

Riding an ATV isn't always a piece of cake. Negotiating rough terrain on an ATV can be a very tricky undertaking. In order to ride safely, avoiding injury and possibly death, you really need to know proper ATV handling procedures and tactics—especially if your path takes you up, down, or across a hill.

### Check out the Terrain

It should go without saying that ATV riders should keep their focus ahead of them as they ride. Get to know your riding area. Assess the variety of terrain available, looking for obstacles or problem areas that may be too much for your equipment or riding skill level. Go slow in unfamiliar areas.

Moderating ATV speed and always looking ahead will help you steer clear of trouble spots. Give riding preference to established pathways or trails that minimize obstacles. When traversing new ground, assess as you go, but proceed slowly and carefully. Maintain absolute control of the ATV at all times.

### Uphill Riding

ATVs are not mountain goats. Some hills are too steep to climb safely on an ATV. Use common sense in planning ahead for an ascent to the top of a hill. Above all else, don't ride uphill as though blindfolded. Know what is ahead of you, either by slowly creeping forward or getting off the unit to inspect firsthand what's ahead. Maintain visibility of the trail forward and to the sides of the chosen travel route.

On steep hills, lean your upper body uphill to maintain stability. *Lee Klancher*

51

As you ride uphill, keep your feet firmly planted on the footrests. Shift into a lower gear to maintain traction before you hit a steep incline. Begin to shift your body weight forward on the seat; then stand in a leaning position with your weight toward the front wheels. This "up and over" front end stance will help maintain the ATV's stability as you climb the hill.

If your climb runs out of steam even in the lowest crawling gear, quickly plan to execute a U-turn. Do not attempt to back down the hill by allowing the ATV to roll backwards. This is a dangerous maneuver. Make the U-turn wide; then proceed downhill at a slow pace using brakes as necessary.

### Going Downhill

The key to safely riding downhill on an ATV is to maintain observation of the terrain ahead as you move forward. Pick as clear a pathway as possible, avoiding obvious obstacles. Riders should shift their weights to the rear of the ATV seat to help keep the unit stable. They also should maintain a firm handlebar grip for control.

Watch your speed going downhill, keeping it in check. Always descend steep pitches in a low gear. As braking becomes necessary, apply brakes gradually, and avoid sudden or abrupt braking—especially to the front wheels—so the ATV won't tip forward.

### Traversing a Hill

Perhaps the trickiest approach on a hill is to traverse one. Again, checking out the terrain ahead of the travel route is important. Avoid slopes with slippery, rough, or loose turf that might cause a sudden loss of control or steering ability. Go slow and concentrate on the task.

When traversing a hill, riders should keep their feet firmly on the ATV footrests. They should also use

Always keep your eye on the trail ahead and anticipate where the riding may be more difficult.

a low gear, maintaining a slow speed and smooth throttle control to adjust to changing terrain. To move across sloping terrain, you often need to "crab" or turn the front wheels uphill a little bit to keep the ATV on track. Holding this front wheel angle will also help prevent the ATV from sliding sideways, especially on steeper slopes.

Always lean your upper body weight into the hill, or to the uphill side of the ATV. This will help avoid a possible sideways tip over. If the ATV should start to tip over toward the downhill slope, turn the front wheels downhill slightly or quickly dismount to the uphill side.

For additional safe riding tips, consult your ATV owner's manual or safety brochure. Taking an ATV riding course is also a good idea. You can also contact the ATV Safety Institute at (800) 887-2887 or visit its Web site (www.atvsafety.org) to obtain a copy of its *Tips and Practice Guide for the All-Terrain Vehicle Rider* safe riding manual.

No matter where you plan to ride, always take an ATV safety course before really getting involved in the sport.
*Lee Klancher*

# Safety Tips for Kids

By Jerrod Kelley

Because children learn by example, adults should always act responsibly and wear the appropriate riding gear.
*Lee Klancher*

Educating children about ATV safety is also very important. Kids need to understand that certain safety guidelines must be followed when operating an ATV, and they especially need to know how to avoid farm accidents on an ATV.

The following organizations offer information on child ATV safety tips and have Web sites that are worth visiting:

### National American Guidelines for Children's Agricultural Tasks (www.nagcat.com)

The National American Guidelines for Children's Agricultural Tasks has a lengthy section of its Web site devoted to ATV safety. Some of the topics covered include appropriate riding apparel, riding tips, and procedures, as well as both adult and youth responsibilities.

NAGCAT says one of the responsibilities that should be taken on by an adult is to ensure that an ATV is in good mechanical condition and that it is of appropriate size before a child rides it. The U.S. government offers these size guidelines for children riding ATVs: 50 cc or below for ages 6 to 11; 50 cc to 90 cc for ages 12 to 15; 90 cc and above for ages 16 and older. Along with these guidelines, adults must make their own decisions whether an ATV is the "appropriate" size (both the engine and physical size) for each individual youth rider.

The NAGCAT site also includes a child riding checklist for adults to fill out. This list ensures that every safety concern is addressed and that a child has the skills needed to operate an ATV safely. It also has "STOP signs" to tell adults when the child is at risk and therefore should not be allowed to operate an ATV.

### Georgia Farm Bureau (www. gfb.org/safety/atv.htm)

One of the Georgia Farm Bureau's safety concerns regarding children and ATV use is that children wear a correctly-sized helmet while riding an ATV. The site asks that the helmets be Department of Transportation –approved and meet Snell Memorial Foundation requirements and the American National Standards Institute guidelines.

The farm bureau also asks adults to follow appropriate age/machine-size restrictions for every child. "Twelve- to 15-year-old drivers who are operating an adult-sized ATV have more than two times the average risk of injury," the bureau reports.

### Farm Safety Day Camps (www.cdc.gov; keywords: ATV safety)

This program asks adults to team up with local organizations to establish a Farm Safety Day Camp for kids. This format attempts to educate children on all farm-relevant safety topics, including ATVs.

Tips include contacting ATV dealers, fire departments, emergency medical services, 4-H and Future Farmers of America representatives, and others related to the agricultural industry for assistance with planning, organizing, and running the camp. One thing that all children should learn when attending the camp is how to choose the proper protective clothing and ATV fit before riding, the site notes. To teach this, the bureau suggests the following: "Practice trying on helmets, gloves, and goggles; measure riders for fit on actual ATVs."

This is a great idea for all children, not just those involved with agriculture. All parents who plan on purchasing an ATV for their children should enter their kids in a program like this. Parents could even form a countywide ATV club that meets to educate youth on ATV safety and operation in all types of situations (from farming to trail riding).

These are two more Web sites with ATV/farm safety information that are worth visiting:

Farm Safety 4 Just Kids: www.fs4jk.org

Wairarapa Rural Education Activities Program: www.waireap.org.nz/school/sam.html

*By Doug Meyer and Cassandra Clawson*

**Time:** 30 minutes to 2 hours

**Tools:** Air gauge, T-handles for bolt check

**Talent:** ★

**Tip:** Do it every time you go on a ride

**Benefit:** Peace of mind

Whether you plan to go on an all-day hunting expedition, an overnight trail-ride, or a week-long adventure, being prepared for your next ATV trip is really what will make the difference between coming back filled up or fed up.

The first step in being prepared for an ATV adventure is to evaluate the aspects of your trip. Is it going to be one day or two? On rugged terrain or on a well-established route? No matter what the answers to these questions are, you should always consider the following:

Whether you're going out on the trail for the day or for a week, you should always make sure your ATV is in good working condition and you have the supplies you need for your trip. *Lee Klancher*

For a camping trip, having the right gear is as important as having the right machine.

- What is the best setup for your ATV on this trek?
- What riding gear and accessories will be needed for the ride?
- What kind of food and beverages should you bring?
- What campsite supplies will be necessary to make the food and provide shelter for those going along?
- How many ATV bags and what size will you need to carry all these items along for the ride?

## ATV Preparation

The first step to preparing your ATV for a multi-mile ride is to check over it thoroughly. First off, inspect the tire pressure. Grabbing the tires with your hands doesn't provide an accurate readout, so use a gauge. And don't roll your eyes at this task! It may seem menial, but it'll only take a few seconds and can save you hours on the trail from waiting for someone to drag your flat-tired ATV out of the woods. While you're down with the tires, do a visual check for cuts or gouges in the tread. If there's a spot on the tire that's been thinned out, replace the tire before hitting the long, dusty trail.

Then, determine if the quad's wheels are tight. Lug nuts and bolts can shimmy loose without notice,

Just like you would on your car, you should always check your tire pressure before going out for a long ride.

so grab a hold of them and twist. If they move in your hand, get out the lug wrench and tighten them. Also, grab the front and rear of each tire and try to rock it on its axle. There shouldn't be any play as you move the wheel, and if there is, you've discovered a worn bearing or loose nut.

OK, now get off the ground and seat yourself on the quad. Press the throttle lever and turn the handlebars to either side. Does the throttle move fluidly and

If your battery and spark plugs aren't working properly, you're definitely going to have problems getting out on the trail.

No matter what kind of trip you are going on, you should check your oil to make sure it's at the right level and doesn't need to be changed. You should also check your gas tank to make sure you have enough fuel to get to your destination.

return quickly when pressure is removed? Good. Next, inspect the throttle cable. If it is securely fastened and undamaged, move on.

Since checking the throttle was so much fun, do the same with the brakes. Pull in the levers to ensure the controls operate smoothly. Then check that the cables are connected in all the right places.

Make sure the ATV has enough oil and gas required for it to run properly. Running out of gas is arguably the most preventable reason for getting stranded. Untwist the cap and peer inside the tank. If you don't see liquid, top it off. And if putting your eye up to a gasoline tank doesn't appeal to you, straddle the ATV and shake it side to side. Fill up the tank if you don't hear much or any see liquid sloshing around inside.

As for the oil reserve, take out the dip stick to check the oil level. Is it low? Is it dark and sludgy? If it's low, put some more in, and if it's dark and gooey, get the oil changed. A seized engine will leave you stranded in the woods and without an ATV, period.

Next, inspect the chain's lubrication (if it has a chain) and adjustment. If it's caked with dirt, clean and completely lubricate it. And if some links are worn out, or the sprocket is missing more teeth than a hockey player, replace them. However, don't replace the chain without replacing the old and busted sprocket and vice versa.

Next, make sure the machine is getting spark and the battery and spark plugs are in working condition. If they aren't, well then, you're not doing a pre-ride inspection—you're doing a no-ride inspection. Charge the battery, and if it doesn't hold a charge, you'll need to buy a new one.

In all of an ATV's massive glory, remember that simple, little nuts and bolts hold your off-roading future in their threads. Jarring trails and rough terrain can shake these important components loose. Look and feel for loose parts before hitting that bumpy trail and periodically retighten major fasteners with a wrench.

If your air filter looks more brown than white, it's time to install a new one. It will do wonders for your quad's performance.

Forgetting to do any of these simple checks could leave you stranded out in the middle of nowhere.

And, just for kicks, why not take a quick peek at the air filter? The engine of a quad needs air just as much as it needs gasoline. If the air filter is dirty, a quick replacement or cleaning will do wonders for the quad's performance. It's also good to check the air filter, if the ATV hasn't been used in a while. Small critters have been known to nest inside air boxes, and a nest of leaves will definitely leave your quad petering out on the trail.

If you are going on a long trail around the Southwest, you should also replace your stock tires with aftermarket ones. Many stock tires do not hold up well over miles of rock-strewn paths.

Also, don't forget to check the fuel shut-off valve once you're out on the trail. If it's in the "off" position, switch it to the "on" position and carry on with your ride.

Next, make sure you have the proper tools to handle any emergencies that may pop up on the trail. Here are some must-have items:
- A tire repair kit
- An extra spark plug
- A tow strap (preferably an installed winch)
- A tool kit (most quads come with one, but you may want to supplement it)

**Riding Gear**
Whether you prepare for a week-long trip across several mountain ranges or just a trip up into the forest, it's always best to be comfortable and protected from the elements. In reality, there is no bad weather, just bad clothing.

Don't be afraid to spend money on quality rain and weather protection. You will be happy you did it if you get caught in a downpour. One other item that can make or break your trip is a good pair of boots. Make sure to get a pair that is insulated, waterproof, and tall enough to walk through a shallow stream without being over-run with water. Some of the better ones on the market are the 8- and 10-inch tall models from Browning or the Magnum from Hi-Tech.

**Riding Accessories**
Many riders disagree about what riding accessories are essential for a trip. Obviously, most would carry a map, but a high-tech rider would insist on a GPS unit. If you miss a turnoff, a GPS unit can give you its exact

location, as well as distances to the nearest towns and camps. It also can measure altitude.

More common technology used on the trail is two-way radio communication. Walkie-talkies keep a group together better and make the ride more enjoyable. Both Collett Electronics and Motorola make units that are perfect to use while ATV riding.

Several other items that are handy to have along include a good pair of binoculars, a camera, and a cellular phone.

### Food and Drink

If there is one guideline that transcends tastes and eating styles here, it is that every ATV adventurer should bring foods that are easy to prepare on a long ride. Among off-roaders, favorites include foods that can come in cups: oatmeal, soup, pasta, beans, and rice. With these, all you need to do is heat up water and, voilá, a meal with no cleanup!

For a nourishing drink, bring along dry Gatorade mix and stir it into your Camelback water backpack so you remain hydrated on the trail. Avoid drinking creek water that could be contaminated.

### Campsite Supplies

To cook food and heat water, you can use the Coleman dual fuel backpack stove. It is designed to work with either unleaded gas or white fuel. To set up a portable table and chairs for your meal, you can use the roll up variety ones that can be found at most major sporting goods stores. While these surely add some bulk to already bulging ATVs, you'll forget all about that when you arrive at camp and get comfortable—really comfortable.

### Miscellaneous Items

Some items, such as trash bags, are things you won't know you need until you need them. Trash bags can be used for more than just carrying your trash out of the woods. They can keep clothes dry and keep clean and dirty clothes separate. Paper towels can prove mighty handy as well, but perhaps the best paper products to take along are baby wipes. These can be used for waterless bathing, for cleaning up cooking gear, as well cleaning dirty parts.

Some of the more obvious things to remember are matches, a flashlight, toilet paper, insect repellent, and eye drops.

### ATV Bags

So how are you going to haul all this stuff anyway? Well, you'll need large bags to carry your food, cooking supplies, and clothing. A medium-sized waterproof duffel bag can carry camping equipment, sleeping pads and bags, as well as rain gear. You'll also want to bring along water and fuel packs that are designed for ATVs.

The right gear may cost a few bucks more than you'd like, but will make the trip so much better—and if you like it, you'll use it again, and again, and again.

<table>
<tr><td>

# PROJECT 14

</td><td>

# Using a Winch

</td></tr>
</table>

By Jerrod Kelley

**Time:** As long as it takes to get unstuck

**Tools:** A winch and tow strap

**Talent:** ★ ★ ★

**Tab:** $300–$500 for winch, $60–$150 for accessory kits

**Tip:** Keep the winch cable taut to prevent it from kinking or fraying

**Benefit:** To protect your investments—the winch and ATV—and to keep yourself safe

Even with the best mud tires, you can get mired in the muck. Even with ground clearance and a full-length skid plate, you can get barred by fallen trees, stopped in the rocks, buried in the snow, and . . . well, you know. But you won't get stuck with a winch.

It's a safe argument that a winch is the most important accessory available to ATV owners. At the same time, many ATV owners are misusing this vital product, and with potentially dangerous consequences.

Warn Industries is full of winching experts, who in this project share information with all ATV lovers out there about the new winches on the market and remind us all about safe winching practices.

## Smart Winching

Even if all you do with your winch is lift and lower a plow blade a few inches, you can do it wrong, damaging your winch, or worse.

Smart winching begins with installing the right equipment correctly. First, if your winch doesn't have a roller fairlead to smoothly guide the cable back onto the winch drum, know that you'll need to pay close attention to spooling in your winch cable to help maintain it.

Having a winch can save you from a whole bunch of trouble. Winching properly can extend the life of the winch and protect you and your ATV from potential harm.

After using a winch in a muddy situation, you should spool out more cable and clean it before respooling.

Taking care of the winch cable is one of the most important elements of smart and safe winching. To do it properly, it's best to "winch in" the cable with a helper operating the switch while you carefully draw tension to the cable as you watch it spool onto the drum. You won't get it on there perfectly like when it came from the factory, but you can keep the cable taut and prevent kinks from fraying the cable. Any sign of frayed or damaged wire means that soon you'll be replacing that cable.

If you use the winch to lift a plow blade, the weight of that blade is not enough to ensure the cable stays taut. The repetitive winch-in and winch-out operation will cause that cable to loosen on the drum and that can mean trouble. If you need to use that winch to rescue a stuck friend, a strong pull on that loosely spooled cable can damage the winch or break a cable. Occasionally, spool the cable out to the end to inspect it for kinks and re-spool it tightly.

If the winch is used strictly for plow lifting, consider shortening the cable to make it specific for that use. Replace the 50-foot cable with a three- to five-foot "snow plowing" cable. It then stays in place on the spool and winds in and out more quickly.

When pulling out a stuck ATV, a rider can help ease the winching process by supplying engine power and steering control. It's also good to freespool the cable to the stuck vehicle because it saves your ATV's battery.

## Winching: 1, 2, 3

Whether winching yourself out of a hole in a self-recovery mode, winching your friend's ATV with your quad-mounted winch, or pulling another object—big log or other—to your ATV, it's easy to do it right.

First, the base unit must be secure and stable. If you're pulling a riding buddy out of a mud hole with your winch, park your ATV in a stable location as far from the stuck quad as possible and set the parking brake. If you're getting yourself out of a jam, you'll need a solid tree or even another ATV that is parked and steady.

Click the winch's clutch into its freespool mode and pull the hook and cable to your helpless pal. You may need to release some tension in the cable before disengaging the winch clutch to freespool.

Attach the hook to a solid frame member on the ATV, not the front bumper or the quad's cargo rack. Even better, use a non-stretch tow strap attached to the quad's trailer hitch or a well-mounted D-ring. All winch manufacturers sell accessory kits that contain the appropriate straps and rings.

If you're pulling with the aid of a tree, wrap a similar strap or tree protector around the tree first. To double the winch's pulling power, use a strap and shackle pulley that allow you to run twice as much cable, pulling the winch hook back to the winching ATV.

Engage the clutch, and winch in to get the cable tight. Now drape a jacket or another object over the tight cable in case it should break while under tension. Keep the winching machine's brake set when you begin the operation. With the ATV running, begin pulling in the cable. Put the ATV in neutral and rev the engine slightly to keep the battery cranking. Let the winch do the work. Don't pull or tow the object with the winching ATV; that stresses the cable and drum. When pulling out a stuck ATV, that machine's driver can assist with engine power and steering guidance.

Use short bursts of winching power, instead of one continuous line pull. This helps keep the winch motor cool and maintains some battery power.

Warn makes self recovery easy with the A2500 and its remote control switch.

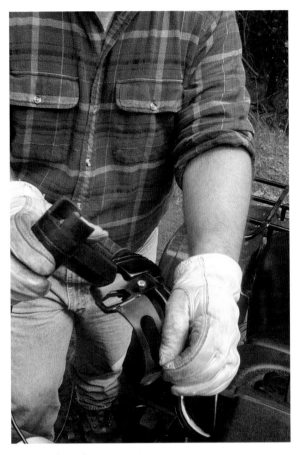

The remote secures into this handlebar-mount bracket (top), and the safety strap (above) makes safe winching easy.

With a successful winching operation complete, take care to re-spool the winch cable correctly. If you've pulled through some mud, you may need to run even more cable out to clean it a bit first. With tension on the hook, pull in the winch cable to get it on the drum evenly and tightly.

## Safe Winching

For a lot of people, a winch is like a screwdriver. You use a screwdriver to turn screws, of course. But you also use it—incorrectly—as a pry bar and a hammer and a scraper and a torque arm and more, even though you know you shouldn't.

Similarly, don't use your winch as a tie-down for securing your ATV to your trailer. Don't use your winch to tow a broken-down ATV to the trailhead. Those are some of the obvious "don't" rules. Read the Safe Reminders list (on page 63) and always winch safely.

## Winch Mounts

Your winch mount can be very important in making your winch easy and safe to use. You can opt for the winch manufacturer's mounting kit, which will be the most affordable option. And since its main purpose is to simply hold the winch, it will likely be the simplest to install.

Many aftermarket innovators have introduced winch mount kits that double as bumpers. Doing double duty, they'll be more expensive and require more installation time. Plus, many of these options are limited to the more popular ATV models. One of these options is an Oxlite bumper/winch-mount kit that gives you a durable steel bumper, plus easy access to your Superwinch; another is an Essex front bumper and winch mount that tucked the Superwinch behind the steel bumper and included a hole for the winch hook and roller fairlead.

A few companies have come up with even more innovative kits that make your winch even more versatile. The Hitch Hopper kit allows you to use a Warn winch off the front or rear of a Honda Foreman ES. The Warn winch and Hitch Hopper combination is hard to beat for versatility. Warn uses thick electrical cables with quick-connect harnesses that allow you to move the winch front and back. It makes winching easy from any location. But when this setup gets dirty, it can have trouble working consistently.

Exposed winch mounts allow you easy access to a winch's "freewheel" switch. And since winch cable often gets knotted up, an exposed mount gives us easy access to the cable spool. A tucked-in mount may look better, and it keeps your quad within its original dimensions.

While machines like the Honda Foreman and Polaris Sportsman will have more winch mount options available, you can find a mount for about any quad.

## Which Winch?

Superwinch models are easy to install, but their handlebar-mounted toggle switches are not always durable enough to handle the electric load. They often stick, then overheat, and break.

Warn has redesigned its rocker switch to be more versatile.

Part of our Warn experience included driving and winching with these 4x4s.

The A2500 winch from Warn is very durable, though it didn't like the repeated mud baths during our tire test. The heavy-duty electrical wires are strong, but the installation of this unit was difficult because of how thick the wires were. The solenoid was not easy to install, either, though it is a nice safety feature once in place. Another nice feature is the Warn winch's wired remote switch. It gives the operator freedom to move away from the winching ATV.

The new Warn 3.0 winch has a 0.9-horsepower motor and is built in a package that's no bigger than Warn's old 2,500-pound winch. The unit is redesigned with a drum that's centered for better balance and torque. Warn added a Teflon coating to the gear train's bushings for less friction. The drum is made of aluminum for resistance to corrosion. And with Warn's cable-retention system, you can change cables easily, even out on the trail if the cable breaks.

Warn has also redesigned its rocker switch. The tiny switch is used with a handlebar-mount bracket that can be positioned in different places on the bars to fit your needs and different machines. The new rocker switch controls were too small, though, as with gloved hands, you would have a difficult time pushing all the small buttons. The versatile switch-mounting mechanism is a nice feature, giving you some variety in where you mount the switch on the bars. It also comes with a remote control on a 10-foot wire.

The winch is also sealed in eight different areas to protect the winch from water and dirt. The winch gears are housed in a steel alloy that protects them from abuse.

This setup gives users easy access to the winch's cable and the freewheel switch.

# Winching Smart Reminders

- Secure the winching vehicle. Never drive the ATV in reverse when winching to try to assist the winch. This pulling combination could overload the cable, rope, or the winch itself.
- Disengage the winch's clutch and use the manual "freespool" mode to extend the cable quickly. This also saves your ATV's battery.
- Stretch a new winch cable to extend its life. Spool almost all the cable out, then wind it back in under a heavy load, at least 500 pounds. This will ensure the inner cable wraps are tight on the drum and will prevent the outer wraps from binding inside the inner ones.
- Drape a coat over the winch cable before beginning the winch operation. In case the cable snaps or the winch hook breaks, weight on the cable will deaden it.

- Wear your helmet and gloves while operating the winch.
- Spooling out as much winch cable as possible allows safer winching and increases the winch's pulling power.
- You can double the power of the winch by rigging a double winch line using a snatch block. Using the nylon sling and snatch block, run the winch cable through the block and back to a secure point on the frame of the ATV.
- Always try to pull the load straight toward the winching vehicle. It is acceptable to start the pull at an angle to get the object in a straight line with your ATV.

# Winching Safe Reminders

- If your rear rack is rated to carry 133 pounds, you're going to want to load it with 200 pounds or more. And if you have a 1,500-pound winch, you'll probably want to pull a 2,000-pound rock. Don't. You'll not only break your winch and maybe your ATV, but possibly hurt yourself.
- Use the right equipment. Superwinch and Warn each sell accessory kits that make winching safe. The Superwinch kit includes a snatch block and pulley, a nylon sling, and a good pair of utility gloves.
- Don't use your winch to lift the deer you shot into your truck. An ATV-mounted winch is not a hoist.
- Don't wrap the winch cable around a tree or ATV bumper. You'll damage the cable, the tree, and the bumper. Use a tree-trunk protector or other non-stretching tow strap.
- Don't attach the winch hook back to the winch cable. The steel hook will harm the winch cable. Use the appropriate straps, D-rings, and shackles to connect the cable and hook safely.

- Don't hold onto the hook or cable while spooling in the winch cable. Tie a rag or cord to the hook to keep your fingers away from the winch drum and spooling cable.
- Don't operate the winch if the cable is all the way out to the bare drum. You can damage the drum or pull the winch cable out completely. The winch cable should be wrapped around the drum at least five times.
- Don't hook one winch to another. This pull will stress the gears inside both winches.
- Don't hold the switch on if the winch motor stalls. If you're using the winch heavily, check the motor for heat, and let it cool down to avoid stalling and overheating.
- These are just a few of the most important rules and techniques for proper winching. Check with the owner's manual of your winch for more information.

| PROJECT 15 | Adding New Clutch Plates and Springs |
|------------|--------------------------------------|

By Jerrod Kelley

**Time:** 2 hours

**Tools:** Socket set, T-handles

**Talent:** ★★★

**Tab:** $100

**Tip:** Carefully disassemble the clutch so you know which order the parts go in

**Benefit:** A better performing clutch

Did you know the clutch is one of the most abused components of an ATV? And did you know the clutch plate assembly is engaged by five interior springs and disengaged by the handlebar-mounted, cable-activated clutch lever? Once the clutch is engaged, the clutch housing and inner friction plates supply power to the steel clutch plates, which are secured to the clutch hub by their inner teeth. The clutch hub is attached to the input shaft and powers the transmission. Without this cohesive unit working together, the clutch may not engage or it may slip. When this happens, it's time to remove the crankcase cover and take a look at the clutch assembly.

If you decide to upgrade your clutch, a good option to consider is the DP Off-Road ATV kit. The DP clutch kit consists of five, non-heavy-duty clutch springs, seven steel pressure plates, and eight friction plates.

## Removal

Before upgrading clutch mods, you need to follow a few procedures. First, drain the engine oil and, if the engine is liquid-cooled, cooling fluid. Second, remove the handlebar-mounted clutch lever assembly. Take the clutch cable out of the holder and then remove the clutch release lever from its mounting bracket. Next, take out the right side engine case cover. To make this easier, take off the foot guard and

After draining the engine oil and cooling fluid (if engine is liquid cooled), remove the handlebar-mounted clutch lever assembly.

The DP Off-Road ATV clutch kit

After taking out the clutch cable, remove the clutch release lever from its mounting bracket.

Make sure you keep track of the two dowels that fit between the crankcase and cover.

When replacing the cover gasket, lightly scrape it off and clean the surface with contact cleaner.

Once you've accessed the clutch, loosen the five bolts that compress the clutch springs and that are on top of the outer pressure plate. Then take the bolts out, as well as the springs and pressure plate.

peg, as well as the tape, or tie-down the rear foot brake. Then, remove the cover bolts and take the cover straight off. Watch for the two dowels that fit between the crankcase and cover; don't lose them. The cover gasket needs to be replaced, so lightly scrape it off and clean the surface with contact cleaner. Now, it's time to access the clutch.

Start loosening the five bolts that compress the clutch springs and are on top of the outer pressure plate. The thrust bearing and washer come off at this point. It's best to use a "criss-cross" pattern, alternating between bolts, to equally relieve pressure from the

springs. Then, take out the bolts, springs, and pressure plate. Before the locknut can come off the shaft, a screwdriver must be used to carefully bend the lockwasher tab off the nut.

Now, remove the clutch plates, friction plates, and clutch hub. Discard the old plates, if they are in bad shape and examine the hub and basket. It's time to start adding the new plates.

Pay attention! DP's kit doesn't require soaking parts in oil prior to installation; some kits will require a bath in engine oil. Also, one of the friction plates is smaller than the other ones; the smaller plate has a "V-notch"

To get the locknut off the shaft, use a screwdriver to bend the lockwasher tab.

and its specific placement within the clutch assembly is first, in this case. Place the clutch boss on a work table with the spline facing up. Install the clutch plates in specific order, starting with the V-notch plate. Next, install a steel plate followed by a friction plate. A cushion spring goes on next, then another steel plate. Continue in this manner until the final friction plate is on.

Align the arrow on the clutch boss with the V-notch on the friction plate. Before reinstalling the clutch hub, align the pressure plate index mark with the one on the pressure plate. From here, it's best to install one clutch spring and bolt to hold together the clutch. Once the clutch boss splines are in line with the main axle splines and friction plate tabs line up with the clutch housing grooves, slide the clutch assembly into the housing. Add a new lockwasher and locknut. The

Install the new clutch plates in specific order, starting with the V-notch plate. Then install a steel plate followed by a friction plate, then a spring, and finally another steel plate. Continue this pattern until the final friction plate is on.

nut—with chamfered side down—should be finger tightened. Secure the clutch and torque the locknut to the specified torque. Next, bed the lockwasher tab so it fits flat on one side of the nut.

Once tightened, remove the bolt and add the remaining clutch springs and then the outer pressure plate. Hand tighten two bolts to add equal pressure to the springs and then add the remaining bolts in a criss-cross pattern. Torque the bolts to correct specification. The clutch plates should not be able to be moved by hand and there shouldn't be any clearance at the back of the cluch. Then, install the bearing and pushrod assembly into the outer pressure plate and reinstall the side cover.

Make certain no dirt or debris entered the clutch assembly and cover while it was removed. Apply a new gasket to the cover and reinstall the dowels. Install the new cover and allow it to seat. After it seats, install a bolt at each end and make certain the cover is properly aligned. Torque the crankcase cover bolts to the specific torque setting found in the owner's manual. Reinstall the clutch cable to the release lever and pull rod assembly. Install the clutch lever assembly to the handlebars.

It's best to examine the clutch cable to see if it needs to be adjusted—especially since you monkeyed with it. Be sure there's enough free play at the lever end. Fire up the engine to see if the tranny properly engages and disengages from the clutch.

Editor's note: We used a Clymer service/repair/ maintenance manual for reference and accuracy.

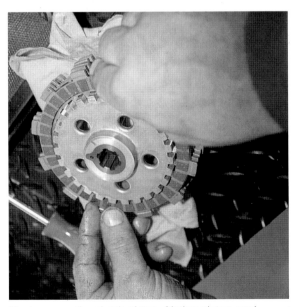

Next remove the clutch plates, friction plates, and clutch hub.

Then align the arrow on the clutch boss with the V-notch on the friction plate.

Slide the clutch assembly into the housing after you have aligned the clutch boss splines with the main axle splines and friction plate tabs.

Once you've put the outer pressure plate on, hand tighten two bolts to add equal pressure to the springs and then add the remaining bolts in a criss-cross pattern. Torque these bolts to correct specification.

# PROJECT 16 | Adjusting Suspension

By Chaz Rice

**Time:** 20 minutes to 2 hours

**Tools:** Spanner wrench

**Talent:** ★★★

**Tab:** Free

**Tip:** Adjust an ATV's suspension according to the load weight or type of terrain it must conquer

**Benefit:** A smoother ride for you

From helping you build a backyard privacy fence to dragging a deer out of the woods or jumping an 80-foot double on a motocross track, ATVs do it all, thanks in part to their suspension. It is a system that is often overlooked by ATV enthusiasts, but it shouldn't be.

## Shock Basics

What do the terms preload, compression, and rebound mean when talking suspension? Now is the time to find out.

ATV owners can choose from many types of shock setups, from stock systems to high-end aftermarket varieties. Most utility ATVs come stock with non-rebuildable, preload-adjustable shocks.

For instance, a 2004 Yamaha Kodiak 450 has three shocks (two up front, one in the rear). All three shocks are preload adjustable via a notched ring below the spring. With a special spanner wrench, an ATV owner can increase or decrease the amount of preload on the shock's spring. Each notch in that silver ring represents a different level of preload in the spring.

What is preload? It is simply the amount of compression in the shock's spring. The more you compress a spring, the more resistance it has. Therefore, the more you adjust the preload, the stiffer the shock gets, and vice versa.

## Par Example

Shocks are designed to work within a certain span of "travel" inside the shock body. The shock design includes a device that helps absorb the bumps; since the size of the shock is limited, this device can only travel so far within the shock body. With a heavy load on the racks, the shock is compressed too much and cannot use its full amount of travel. Take some of that

1. Here is what is referred to as a remote reservoir for adjusting the shock's compression.
2. The preload adjuster ring on this front shock is used to set sag and prevent diving in corners.
3. At the bottom of this rear shock is the rebound adjuster.

space away by decreasing the amount it can travel and bad things happen.

Two of the most common troubles are decreasing the life of the shock and damaging the internal moving parts from bottoming out the shock too much. And since most stock shocks are not rebuildable, once ruined, you will have to buy new ones from the manufacturer or the aftermarket—and that isn't cheap.

Let's say you are going to carry 40-pound bags of cement on a Kodiak 450. Like everything, there is a right way and a wrong way to do this. The wrong way is piling the bags on the racks and taking off. The front and rear ends of the ATV keep getting closer to the ground as more weight is added to the racks. When you do this, you are taxing the suspension and preventing it from doing its job—absorbing bumps and keeping the ride smooth.

The right way is to pay attention to the preload adjuster. Each bag weighs 40 pounds. Start loading the rack and you can clearly see the suspension trying to work, but it is losing ground.

For correct preload with loaded racks, make sure to adjust the shocks—left and right—to the same amount of preload. With the springs properly preloaded, as the bags are piled onto the racks, the suspension doesn't compress as much and retains the proper ride height.

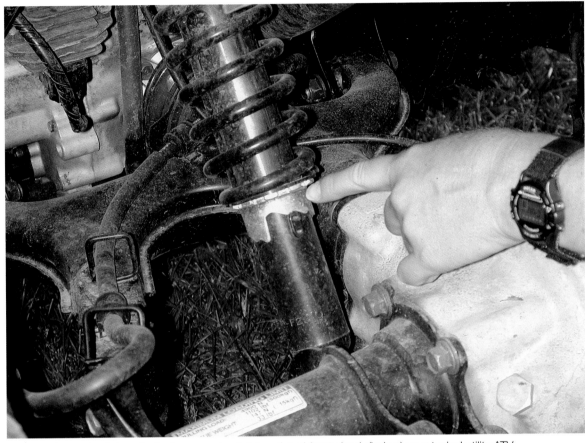

Here are the preload rings for both a rear shock (above) and front shock (below) on a typical utility ATV.

Now, the ride is smooth because the spring is doing its job and the shock doesn't bottom out when the racks are loaded. But once the bags are removed, the ride will be harsh because each bump will be transferred to the rider due to the stiffness of the spring. Without the extra load on the racks, the opposite is happening to the shock. Instead of the travel being forced to the bottom of the shock because of the load, the travel is forced to the top.

When the racks are empty, return the preload to its normal level. And since we all weigh different amounts—and the manufacturers can't build a shock personalized to your weight—you can use the preload adjustment to tailor the ride to your liking.

## Custom-Tailored Suspension

Now that the preload is out of the shocks, do you feel how the ATV is responding? Chances are it will dive in the front and bounce when going across bumps.

Take your spanner wrench and increase the preload a notch at a time on each shock. Ride in the same area and go across the same bumps. The ride should improve. Again, make more adjustments and repeat. Set a good base level where the ride is comfortable to your style; make the suspension work for you! Take some time to dial it in and you will notice an improvement.

### Sport Quads

While most utility ATVs only have preload-adjustable shocks in both front and rear, sport quad suspensions are more high tech. ATVs such as Honda's 400EX, Suzuki's Z400, and Yamaha's Raptor have front shocks that are both non-rebuildable and preload-only adjustable, but rear shocks that are preload ajustable, compression- and rebound-adjustable, and can be rebuilt. These are designed to suit a variety of riding styles.

You can make adjustments to the front shocks using the adjustment tips discussed earlier in this project, but keep in mind that when you make adjustments on a sport quad, it will react in a different way than a utility quad. This is a machine designed for high-speed riding and its suspension reacts differently on a high-speed run.

Before making any adjustments to your ATV's suspension, though, record the initial settings. Also keep a log to track settings when testing. This is helpful when trying to diagnose handling problems.

### Compression

Compression is the adjustment that determines how fast the shock will compress when hitting a bump. The shock's compression adjustment is located on the shock body or on the remote reservoir and is adjustable by "clicking" the screw in or out.

The faster the compression, the faster the shock travels toward bottoming out. Hit a bump with too fast of a compression rate and the ride will feel mushy and springy; the shock will want to bottom out too much. Slow down the compression, and every bump will be transferred to the rider, making the ride harsh and rough.

### Rebound

Rebound is how fast the shock returns to its normal ride height. This adjustment is found on the bottom of the shock and is adjustable by "clicking" the screw in or out.

With too quick of a rebound setting, the shocks will make the ATV buck. The shock will spring back rapidly and could send the rider over the bars or slam the seat into the rider's butt.

A shock with the rebound set too slow will "pack up" in the bumps. Packing up is when the shock cannot travel back to its ideal ride height and each successive bump takes more and more travel away from the shock until it can no longer absorb any bumps.

### Putting It All Together

The key to suspension tuning on a sport quad is putting all these adjustments together—and this is neglecting different internal shock valving or different spring rates! With all these factors to consider, one can see why a suspension tuner can charge outrageous rates for his expertise. The key is to make small adjustments at one time.

Since most sport quad front shocks have only a preload adjustment, the adjusting stops there, and once the shock's useable life is used up, that is it for the shock. We have seen riders blow out front shocks after one race. Stock front shocks are not meant for all-out racing.

The rear shock can be rebuilt and is fully adjustable. Again, remember, do small adjustments one at a time to be safe. For jumps, slow the compression down. This will make slow riding more harsh, but the shock will absorb the large jumps. For woods racing, the ride should be plush; speed the compression. Hit some bumps and jumps and have a good set of whoops—bumps roughly two feet tall and spread across a long run—to test the adjustments. Adjusting shocks can be a maddening experience, but if done properly, your ride will improve.

# PROJECT 17 | Replacing Brakes

By Chaz Rice; Wrenching by Rolly Bartell

**Time:** 1 hour

**Tools:** Lug wrench (a pneumatic wrench is preferable), exhaust spring puller, contact cleaner, Allen wrench, needlenose pliers

**Talent:** ★★★

**Tab:** $40

**Parts:** Cotter pins, brake components (pads)

**Tip:** Don't touch new brake pads with greasy hands; wear gloves!

**Benefit:** The ability to slow down and stop your ATV

**Complementary Project:** Brake bleeding

ATVs still have drum brake setups, although drums are becoming more rare. Honda still swears by them and included drums on its top-of-the-line Rincon. For this demonstration, we are replacing brake drums on a Rubicon.

It is now well into the riding season and those brakes that felt mushy earlier this year now feel downright dangerous. Last year you ran in a lot of mud, and this season has been no different. Listen up: You need to respect your brakes and respect them now. The little bit of pad material left on your brake shoes will fail at the most inopportune moment—guaranteed.

Changing drum brakes isn't as hard as you might think. In fact, it is so easy that you really have no excuse. Still, however, we at *ATV Magazine* get questions on

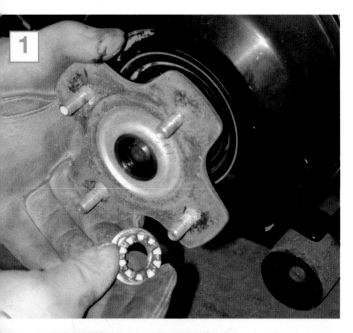

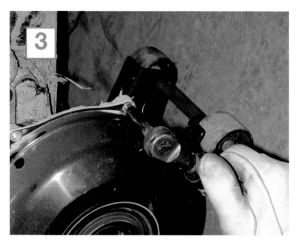

3. Remove the drum cover bolts. It helps to have a pneumatic wrench for this step, but cranking them loose with a socket and ratchet works too.

4. Once you have the cover off, peer into the dark and dusty world of a brake drum. See that dust? That was once your brake pad.

5. There are two things you can do at this point. The first is check for wear. Measure the pad material left on the shoe and check it in the specifications of your machine's owner's manual. If the material left is out of specification, replace away. The other option is to replace the pads regardless of a measurement.

6. Now comes the fun part. To remove the shoes, you will have to pull the springs, which attach the shoes to the housing. The best way to do this is with an exhaust spring puller. If you do not have one, pliers can work too, but not as well. The springs can be pretty taut, so be careful when doing this. Some shoes come with new springs, some don't. If you have to reuse the old springs, inspect them for damage.

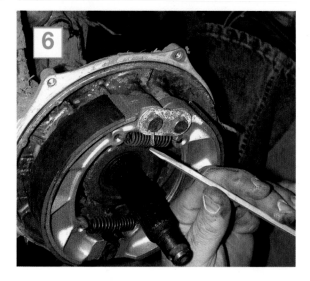

changing brake pads and shoes all the time. Here is the step-by-step guide to this easy, do-it-yourself operation:

1. Remove the right rear wheel. This exposes the drum housing, which is clearly visible. Next remove the hub nut and the cotter pin. Do not reuse cotter pins—always have a supply on hand. They are available at any hardware store. Cotter pins are very important for making sure the hub nut does not back off and come loose. This can lead to, among other things, your tire flopping off.

2. On the Rubicon we were working on, the drum housing is located just inside the wheel, making access easy. Some manufacturers locate the housing closer to the center of the axle.

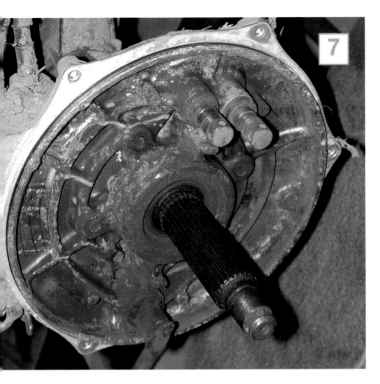

8. Locate both the positioning pins and activating pin. They are easy to find—the shoes mount to the positioning pin, and moving the brake lever or pedal moves the activating pin. Lube these with brake grease. This ensures smooth operation. Make sure not to get any grease on the new shoes or drum.

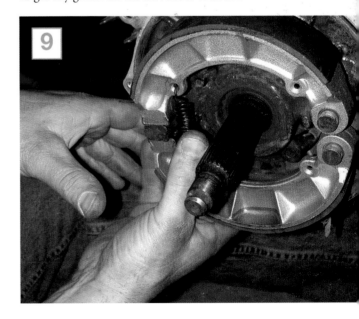

7. After removing the shoes, wipe the drum clean and remove all the accumulated brake dust. Spray contact cleaner and blow compressed air to remove dust. It is important to do this because it will prolong the life of the new pads. If you use compressed air, wear a dust mask or respirator. You don't want that brake dust in your lungs.

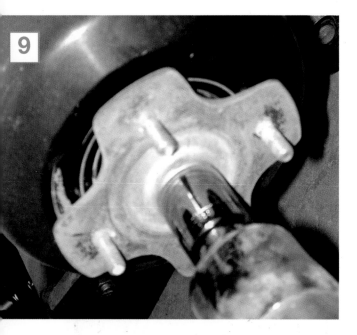

9. Mount the shoes in the reverse order of how they came out. Install the springs and put the drum back on the axle. Then reinstall the housing cover. You are almost done.

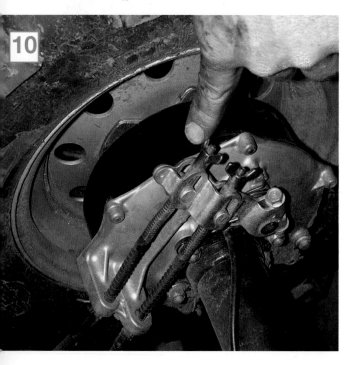

10. With new pads, you will have to readjust the "feel" of the brakes. This is accomplished with the brake adjusters located just outside the drum housing. These wing nuts allow you to adjust free play in the brake lever. Usually a fourth to a half of an inch is enough free play.

## Disc Brakes

Disc brakes are a little different than drum brakes, but no more difficult to work on. In some ways, they are easier. Disc brakes work exactly like the ones on your car. The system consists of a brake rotor, a brake caliper, brake pads, and some sort of hydraulic activation via a lever to close the caliper. About 90 percent of sport quads feature disc brakes and more and more utility models are switching to them.

The first step in disc maintenance is to remove the wheel. This exposes the caliper and rotor.

A good tip is to loosen the bolts holding the pad to the caliper before removing the caliper from the mounting bracket. This allows you to get better leverage on the pad bolts.

Removing the caliper is simple. Locate the three or four Allen bolts holding the caliper to the mounting bracket. Sometimes the bolts are pretty tight, so wear gloves to avoid bloody knuckles. Once you have the caliper off, remove the pads from the caliper. Sometimes the pads will squeeze together if you move the hydraulic lines around. This activates the piston behind one of the pads. Simply push them apart with a flathead screwdriver.

Now that the caliper and pads are off, inspect the rotor. How does it look? Are there gouges in it? If so, you may need a new one. For sport quad enthusiasts, this is a great time to save some weight by investing in a lighter rotor.

Take your new brake pads and install them in the caliper. Make sure not to touch them with your greasy hands. If you do, clean them with contact cleaner—not WD-40!

Mount the caliper back to the mounting bracket and tighten everything. Test to make sure that the new pads are not restricting the movement of the rotor.

## Brake Bleeding

Servicing disc brakes is also a great time to "bleed" the brake system. It is not a priority, but if your brakes feel mushy—or it has been more than two years since the system has been bled—take the time to do it.

Use the fluid the manufacturer recommends. Buy enough of it to completely flush the system. You will need more for the front brake system.

Along with fluid, you will need clear rubber tubing with a diameter of about 8–10 millimeters (large enough to fit the bleeder valve on each caliper), a 10-millimeter crescent wrench, a container to catch the old brake fluid, and a buddy's help.

On each caliper, you will find a bleeder valve. Attach the tubing to this valve and make sure it is a tight fit. Feed the tubing into the jar or whatever you are using to catch the bled fluid.

Locate the brake fluid reservoir and remove the top cap. You should see fluid. If you don't, your brakes aren't working. It is this fluid that activates the brake pads.

This is where the buddy comes in. Have him pump and hold in the brake lever while you open the bleeder valve. Do not pump up the system a ton. Just do it enough to force fluid out the bleeder valve.

You will have to alternate opening the bleeder valve with pumping the system to maintain pressure.

While the old fluid is being purged from the system, keep the reservoir topped with fluid. If you do not, you will introduce air into the system and will defeat the purpose of a brake bleed.

Make certain not to spill brake fluid, new or old, on any painted parts. Brake fluid eats through paint in seconds. It's also a good idea to wrap an old rag or sponge around the reservoir to catch spills before they can drip onto your quad's paint.

The old fluid will look, well, old. Purge it from the whole system until new fluid starts flowing from the bleeder valves. Close the bleeder valve and hit the trail.

Most sport quads, and a growing number of utility ATVs, have disc brakes. *Lee Klancher*

| **PROJECT 18** | Fixing a Flat Tire |

By Jerrod Kelley

**Time:** 15 to 20 minutes

**Tools:** Tire repair kit, inflating device

**Talent:** ★★

**Tab:** $15–$50

**Parts:** Tire repair kit

**Tip:** The better the kit, the better the repair

**Benefit:** It will get you back to the trailer

An expected flat tire can "deflate" your riding adventure in a quick hurry. But how many of us can say we always carry a tire repair kit with us on our off-road trips? We admit it: We're just as guilty as every other ATV rider out there who doesn't always fully prepare for a ride, but with all the easy-to-use repair kits out there, none of us really has a good excuse for getting stranded by a flat anymore.

**Safety Seal**

This portable 10-piece tire repair kit can fit in a backpack, storage box, or rack bag, and it will fix almost any type of puncture to your ATV tire. Safety Seal designed the kit to fix a flat and get ATV riders back on the trail, not limping back to camp.

Oddly, for this test, we purposely made a flat tire on our test quad. To do this, we drilled a 1/4-inch bit into our rear tire and allowed it to deflate. In most situations, you will either have to find the puncture using soapy water (watching for bubbles) or locate the item in the tire that created the flat. While you remove the item, note the object's puncture path. Once this step is complete, insert a Safety Seal plug (the sticky brown strips in the protective paper) into the split-eye

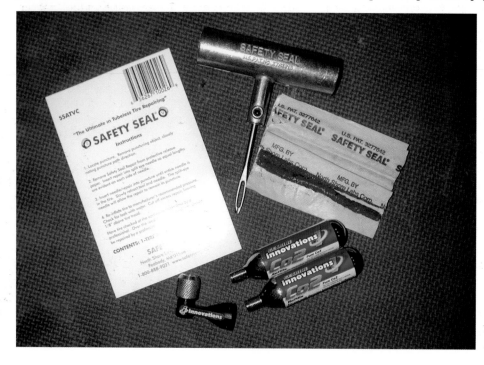

The Safety Seal tire repair kit is as effective as a spare.

Once the puncture is located, use the T-handle tool and repair strip to seal it.

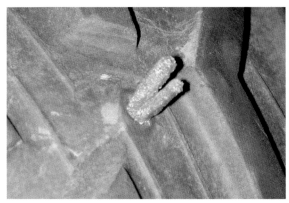

Once sealed, the tire is ready for some $CO_2$.

The Microflate tool and $CO_2$ cartridges make tire inflation simple.

needle of the T-handle tool. Make sure the repair strip has an equal amount on each side of the eyelet.

The next step is to "push" the entire needle and repair strip into the puncture hole in the tire. From there, slowly pull out the needle. The split eye design will let the repair strip stay inside the tire, and you should see two ends of the strip sticking out of the puncture hole. Trim the excess at about an eighth of an inch from the tire.

Now the hole is repaired, but the tire is still flat. To fix this problem, screw one of the supplied $CO_2$ cartridges onto the L-shaped Microflate tool. By twisting the cartridge into the tool's threaded base, you puncture the canister, but don't allow the $CO_2$ to escape.

Now, attach the blue part of the dual-nozzle Microflate tool to the tire's valve stem. This part will press on to some valves and screw onto others. Once you've done this, partially unscrew the $CO_2$ canister from the threaded base until you hear the flow of gas and see the tire inflate. This step requires both supplied cartridges of $CO_2$ and adds six psi to the now-inflated tire.

When pulled, the repair plug is held up; it didn't "bust" loose or create an air leak. Even after testers jumped up and down on the tire to see if the repair strip could be loosened, the tire kept its air. Then they got back on the Yamaha Grizzly and took it for a run—accelerating, stopping quickly, and making tight turns. Still, the Safety Seal repair strip stood strong.

**Stop & Go**

This kit ($20) has a snazzy little pouch that contains all the necessary elements for tire repair. It includes tire plugs, a reaming tool, an insertion tool, rubber cement, and two canisters of $CO_2$ with a hose to connect them to the tire.

This Stop & Go kit's snazzy little pouch holds everything you need to fix your tire while out on the trail.

Using an insertion tool, you'll find it easy to plug a tire leak with these string plugs.

The rubber cement keeps the plugs firmly planted.

The kit includes easy instructions—a bonus for a high-stress, flat-tire situation. The reaming tool (the spiral screwdriver) is used to clean out any orphaned rubber or miscellaneous debris from the hole. It did its job swimmingly.

The tire plugs are the string type, which look like small strips of beef jerky but don't smell nearly as inviting at the meat treat. The string plug was easy to peel from the plastic sheeting and, most importantly, it plugged the hole easily. The rubber cement was gooey, as it should be, and kept the plug firmly planted in the tire after installation.

Unfortunately, the inflation system included in the Stop & Go kit leaves a lot to be desired. The threads on the $CO_2$ canisters got mashed while in transit. Trying to screw canisters with mangled threads into the inflator isn't easy. Filling the tire is also a chore. During our test, all the $CO_2$ leaked out before the container was screwed tight. We were unable to direct the flow into the tire, even after we devised ways to get the inflation kit assembled and to the tire quickly. So the Stop & Go sealed the hole in the ATV's tire, but did nothing to reinflate the tire. Obviously, the system needs some tweaking, but the company has half the tire repair equation right.

## Genuine Innovations

Genuine Innovations offers a standard tire repair kit ($30), as well as two other, more expensive, ATV tire repair kits. The standard kit comes contained in a nifty, semi-padded pouch and includes all the goodies needed to plug a puncture in rubber: string-type plugs, a reaming tool, an installation tool, rubber cement, tube patches, a scuffer, three canisters of $CO_2$, and an inflator.

This kit's string-type plug is identical to the Stop & Go kit. Unlike the Stop & Go kit, though, the Genuine Innovations plugs are difficult to separate from the plastic sheeting. This is an annoyance in the garage, and a larger pain on the trail. But the reaming tool works well, as well as the plug installation tool.

This kit also has a handy inflating device that secures the $CO_2$ cartridge, then allows the seal to be broken and expels the gas into the tire. While the cartridge only semi-inflates a flat, it does provide enough air that you can get your quad back to civilization safely, at least.

Genuine Innovations has a variety of tire repair kits, including this standard one that retails for $30.

Taking a drill to your tire? Unthinkable. That's what we at *ATV Magazine* did, though, to test these products.

The Quad Boss inflation kit costs $18.

### Quad Boss

The Quad Boss kit's contents vary a bit from the previous two kits'. This kit ($18) includes threaded nylon plugs that screw into the tire's hole. It also includes two jars of glue, an insertion screwdriver, and a can of air. It lacks a reaming tool, but you won't really miss it with the nylon-type plugs.

The plugs impressively seal a tire hole. They screw in with the adhesive acting as a lubricant and form a tight and secure bond. After screwing them in, you can't help but notice that they look solid and reliable.

The inflation system in this kit is also a winner. It attaches to the valve easily and fills the tire at a controllable pace without waste.

The kit's inflation system attaches to the valve easily and fills the tire well.

By Jerrod Kelley

**Time:** 15 minutes to 1 hour

**Tools:** Basic tool kit with socket wrench

**Talent:** ★★

**Tab:** $200

**Parts:** Exhaust kit

**Tip:** Pay attention to the fitment

**Benefit:** For hunting, having a quiet ATV is a good thing

**Complementary Project:** Adding hunting accessories to your ATV

Grizzly bears are most known for their giant size and brute strength, but they are also known for their deafening roar. In the ATV market, the ever-popular Yamaha Grizzly is one force to be reckoned with. It's known for its engine, agility, and looks . . . and of course its roar.

For those riders who need to somehow tame this beast a little around the neighborhood or out on trails closer to civilization, adding an exhaust quieter might be a necessary project.

At around $200, the ATV Stealth Exhaust is worth the price for its reduced sound levels.

**The Kit**

ATV Stealth Exhaust, manufactured by Kolpin Outdoors Inc., is a super-quiet, high-flow, bolt-on, four-stroke exhaust system with a USDA Forest Service–approved spark arrestor. This exhaust is supposed to quiet your stock ATV exhaust by reducing the exhaust noise by up to 50 percent.

Kolpin notes that installation is based on "personal preference" (read: riding style, rear design of machine) and can be done several ways by using the universal mounting kit. The company also says its system fits any brand or model quad with a four-stroke powerplant.

If you follow the "direct mount" directions for bolting the system on the Yamaha Grizzly, you will need to add a 1.5-inch male bushing on the stock outlet and attach the Stealth Exhaust inlet to the stock outlet. Orange high-temperature silicone is recommended on all connections for a tighter, quieter seal. When connecting the Stealth unit to the Grizzly rear rack for support, attach two rubber-coated mounting clamps and two wrap-around universal mount muffler hangers on the Yamaha's rear rack. Before tightening this setup, measure the hangers and cut the extra length off with a power saw.

Once you find the right length, tighten the clamps and hangers and the U-bolt clamp to the stock end cap. Then add about a 12-inch section of Flex pipe to the Stealth system's outlet, pointing it to the ground and tightening it with another U-bolt clamp. If you use flexible tubing, it also will help reduce noise levels and will "flex" when it comes in contact with obstacles.

The Stealth Exhaust system does not restrict the use of the rear rack or block the Grizzly's rear brake light, but the Stealth unit gets hot. Because it is more exposed, unlike the stock exhaust, use caution at the rear of your quad.

In this test, the Stealth system considerably reduced the Grizzly's exhaust sound levels. Though this Yamaha wasn't overly loud to begin with, it is now much quieter, even at full throttle. This should be a plus for anyone with peace-loving neighbors. For hunting trips and areas with noise restrictions, you may just surprise people when you sneak out of the woods.

## What about Power?

Kolpin also claims that the Stealth Exhaust "in some cases" increases performance on your ATV. To see if this was true, we put the Stealthy Grizzly on a Dynojet dynamometer to compare its horsepower numbers to stock.

The Grizzly with stock exhaust produced 29.8 horsepower. The horsepower numbers for the Stealth Grizzly dropped off almost 2 horsepower, to 28.2 horsepower. Our technical editor said the Stealth Exhaust created too much back pressure for the Grizzly, ultimately reducing the horsepower numbers.

This loss of power isn't always a negative thing, though. Because the pipe is so quiet and bolts on in less than 15 minutes, this is a minimal drop in power and the kit is a good investment. Now you have the convenience of having your stock horsepower, when needed, or a quieter system with another spark arrestor and good horsepower numbers. And it's affordable too, at around $200.

Installation is versatile and can take as little as 15 minutes.

## PROJECT 20 | Adding Cruise Control

By Chaz Rice

**Time:** Two to three hours

**Tools:** Electrical supplies, tool kit

**Talent:** ★★★★★

**Tab:** $893

**Parts:** The QuadCruise kit includes all parts

**Tip:** Take time to follow the directions

**Benefit:** For those who need precise throttle control, this is the ticket

Look, Ma, no thumb! That's the advantage of having cruise control on your ATV—no need to operate the throttle, just let your thumbs take a break. What a perfect way to enhance a Sunday afternoon ATV ride.

QuadCruise by Australian-based Motorcycle Setup is one cruise control on the market that can be used for a number of applications, from farm chores to recreational hobbies. You know how cruise control works on a car, right? Turn it on, set the desired speed, and just cruise down the outstretched asphalt ribbon. Well, the QuadCruise works in much the same way. The control box has all the buttons your Chevy pickup has to control and regulate cruise control. There are a few distinct differences, though.

Installation took longer than expected, but once that was finished the QuadCruise proved its worth.

One is that the QuadCruise is only for an ATV (although a streetbike version is available). Two is that the cruise will work at low speeds only, to keep things safe. Three? It works at speeds as low as four miles per hour, but features both acceleration and deceleration capability in small increments, just like on an automobile. The QuadCruise also allows the user to regulate spray control on an electric sprayer. In essence, it combines accurate ground speed control with accurate spray delivery. It's perfect for people who have to deliver herbicide or pesticide accurately.

The QuadCruise is set up distinctively for each particular model. Depending on which model you install the unit on, the QuadCruise senses speed differently. Each kit comes with parts to mount it to your particular machine.

Installing the unit does take some time—well, a lot of time. Look to spend two to three hours making sure everything is in proper working order. The installation instructions are good and provide detailed photographs to facilitate the installation. All the parts you need are included in the kits.

Items to install include the following: a computer box that is the brains of the QuadCruise, a vacuum reservoir and actuator to regulate the throttle, and the switch and control box. Each kit also comes with a loom of wires, which connect everything together. The most time-consuming part of the kit is the wiring, as well as determining where to place the components so they'll stay dry. Some kits also come complete with a speed sensor that is mounted on the machine to relay speed to the "black box."

The control box mounts to the handlebar and is simple in design. It has four buttons that allow the user to control speed, set speed, and spray delivery. With a push of the "set" button, everything comes to life and the unit starts working. The control box mounts on the handlebar with a sturdy mounting clamp. It has four switches and appears to be protected from the elements.

Put simply, the CPU monitors ground speed at all times, and when the "set" button is pushed, the computer takes a read of what the speed is—not in miles per hour, but rather what the sensor is sending to the unit in pulses of electricity. Then the unit automatically adjusts speed using the vacuum actuator, which controls the throttle to maintain the pulse frequency at the same rate. Just like a car, if the pulses slow down, the computer gives more throttle, and vice versa. It happens so quickly, you don't even realize all the changes being made.

We tested the QuadCruise at both low and moderate speeds and found it to hold speed no matter how rough the land and how much grip the tires could find. The only place it might have problems is in mud and going up steep inclines, like out of a ditch for example.

The safety feature worked on the second test, but strangely, not on the initial test. On the initial test, the cruise control engaged at a high rate of speed. But this did not happen during subsequent tests. At slow speed, however, the unit worked great—definitely its selling point.

As for the QuadCruise being durable, the Sportsman 500 we tested it on sank—yes sank—in a mud hole. The cruise still worked and all was well with the unit. The CPU was mounted pretty high on the ATV to protect it, but the sensors and vacuum pieces still worked. Only time will tell if the unit can withstand the torture test and if the moving pieces can get caked with silt and still work, however.

In all, this is a product a small farmer who utilizes an ATV for the majority of his work should consider. It is a neat unit and a great idea.

The QuadCruise even withstood a swim at *ATV Magazine*'s R&D center.

# SECTION 3
# ON THE HUNT

| PROJECT 21 | Using Security Locks |
|---|---|

Staff Report

**Time:** 15 minutes

**Tools:** Half a brain

**Talent:** ★

**Tab:** $70–$130

**Parts:** 20-millimeter barbed wire

**Tip:** In high-theft areas, use a second lock to keep your ATV grounded

**Benefit:** Better safe than sorry

Maybe securing an ATV while you're off hunting hasn't been a major concern in the past because no one would want to steal your 1980 Big Red three-wheeler. But what about your spanking new $7,000 Honda Rubicon? With the growing popularity of quads, almost every machine is a thief-worthy target, especially the new ATVs—from sport quads to big bore 4x4s.

Even those of us at *ATV Magazine* were recent victims of ATV theft when one of ours was stolen from a staffer's backyard. So to make sure your newest toy doesn't suffer the same fate, here are some ways to secure your ATV the next time you have to leave it unattended.

**Surelock Wheel-Lock**

Manufactured by Therring Innovations, this wheel lock is intended to prevent roll-off theft. It attaches in less than five minutes to any ATV's rear wheels. To do this, set the plastic-coated bent ends in the rims of your ATV's tires and select a desired hole in which to latch the adjusting link; then tighten and padlock.

As for the devices' effectiveness, it does slow an ATV to a head-jarring halt within one full revolution of the tires. It also works without damaging the quad and without self-destructing.

**Above and right:**
The Surelock Wheel-Lock, which utilizes a wheel-clamping locking system, is one solid security device that's portable to boot. It's best to clamp both the front and rear wheels.

Ideal for home security, the Hitchin' Post from CDS Inc. is also portable and secure.

If a thief tries to roll an ATV off by its front tires, he usually ends up only being able to move it a few feet due to the machine's weight. Though extremely heavy for just one adult, this task could be handled by three or four people rather easily and quickly. That's why you should use two Surelock Wheel-Locks at once; one on the front wheels and one on the rear.

## Hitchin' Post

Think of this security mechanism as a corkscrew anchor for the ground. Though this lock looks gimmicky, there's much more to it than tricks. The Hitchin' Post is a small auger-like device with a bicycle U-lock connected to the top end. It is designed to secure an ATV with its anchor drilled two-feet deep into the ground and the U-lock attached to a sturdy segment of the quad (we suggest the frame).

The product's success depends on where you choose to screw it into the ground. Don't try to screw it in near a large tree. During our test, that move wasn't successful. The Hitchin' Post stopped drilling down after 1.5 feet—probably tree roots or hidden rocks stopped its progress. You will also find it difficult to screw the Hitchin' Post into the ground if the soil is dry or frozen. In fact, locating the best type of ground to screw this lock into is far from simple. Sand and mud won't hold it and rocky/gravel-like soil might not work either. Also, you'll need a lot of energy to get the Hitchin' Post all the way into the ground manually.

Once it's all the way in the ground, however, the Hitchin' Post works well. During testing, we tried to uproot it by revving up a Honda Foreman, but the lock stayed secure—even though it's U-bar did bend a bit in the process.

Sure, a thief could bring along some tools or a shovel and dig the Hitchin' Post out of the ground, but then he would be left with the problem of separating the lock from the quad. The quad won't run if the device obstructs its operation. To make it even harder to separate the quad from the Hitchin' Post, you can use a system of locks with cables and an anchoring device as a secure point in which to fasten all the other locks. A better bet would be to secure the Hitchin' Post in concrete for the ultimate security method at home.

The Hitchin' Post is also beneficial because it can be transported from place to place. Just remember to choose your ground wisely and attach it to something solid on the quad.

## Kryptonite

When selecting a security device for your ATV, the first lock that comes to mind—especially if you've ever owned a bicycle—is the Kryptonite U-lock. Luckily, the Kryptonite company, as part of its expansion into the motorcycle and ATV industry, has created a small U-shaped disc lock that fits through an ATV's disc brake and prevents the vehicle from being driven or rolled away. The only problem, though, is finding a place on the trail that will serve as an anchor for the lock that is made of 13-millimeter hardened "Kryptonium" steel. If you can't find such an anchor, link two quads together so they are harder to run off with.

To ensure further safety of your ATV, you should add a 20-millimeter barbed wire cable to your U-lock.

The cable, a heavy-duty security cable made of plastic-coated braided steel, has a loop on one end that enables it to encircle the frame of the ATV and then connect to the U-lock.

The Kryptonite lock is impressive in its flexibility. It can be taken on hunting trips, trail rides, or camping adventures without consuming too much storage space on the ATV. And while these security devices aren't the cheapest products available, they will protect your quad and that makes them well worth the money.

### Maximum Security LockDown

Initially created as a motorcycle security system, the Maximum Security LockDown—from Australian manufacturer Taffynackles Inc.—now works on ATVs just as well.

To install the system, first select the surface or structure the ATV will be secured to. These could include a concrete floor, wall, trailer, truck bed, snowmobile trailer, or whatever. Next attach the Maximum Security LockDown base ring to the structure using three long, heavy-duty bolts. For bolting the ring to wooden objects, use lag bolts. For concrete applications, use steel masonry hardware (which is included in the kit). The kit is milled from a solid steel bar and then case hardened and chromed for ultimate durability and design.

During testing, we chose two anchor points for the Maxim Security LockDown: a utility trailer with an inch-thick wooden floor and a large willow tree. On the trailer, the lag bolts were too long for the thin wooden floor. In order to fix this, we placed a two-by-four underneath the selected bolting area to ensure

It's the simplest system to use and transport; plus the Kryptonite Evolution 2000 ATV U-Lock and barbed wire combination is lethal at stopping thieves. It isn't cheap, however, and works best when locked to a secure anchor point.

The Maximum Security LockDown isn't the most portable unit and does require the need for tools, but it is strong.

the hold and to prevent the bolts from being exposed below the trailer floor. Once set up, the LockDown did not budge—even after a 'thief' tried several times to break the lock from the floor.

On the willow tree, we used a Kryptonite cable to secure our ATV to the tree and the ring. Again, the 'thief' tried to break the lock—this time using a long, heavy steel bar to jimmy it apart. The bar did bend, but did not break.

The Maximum Security LockDown comes in two different sizes and works with virtually all cable locks, padlocks and chains, cables and fork locks, and U-locks.

## Which Is Best?

We recommend the Kryptonite locks. They are portable, versatile, and simple to use. You can use these locks for your ATV, watercraft, snowmobile, garden tractor, snowblower, or whatever. The Wheel-Lock system is also very easy to use, as is the Hitchin' Post—if you can find solid ground to drill it in. The Maximum Security LockDown's only drawback is its need for a drill—that's why it would work best as a home security device. Use concrete as your anchor here.

# PROJECT 22 | Turning an ATV into a Portable Hunting Blind

By Blake Stranz

**Time:** 1 to 2 hours

**Tools:** Basic tool kit

**Talent:** ★★★

**Tab:** $650–$800

**Parts:** The rapid blind kit from Arctic Cat and an MRP-equipped Arctic Cat ATV

**Tip:** Make sure to follow directions

**Benefit:** To bag the game, you need to conceal your quad

**Complementary Project:** Adding hunting accessories to your ATV

One of the most dreaded chores hunters face is the walk back to the hunting spot after stashing the ATV. Quads are a great tool for getting all the necessary gear to the site, but then what do you do with them? Many hunters try to camouflage them with natural material; others drive far off site, then have to hoof it back to their hunting post.

But what if you had a blind that attached to the machine? What if it could camouflage an ATV, two hunters, and a dog? If that sounds like a dream setup for your hunting days, Arctic Cat may have something for you.

The Rapid Blind attaches to Arctic Cat's multi-rack platform system. It slips into the multi-rack platform (MRP), where it is held securely by the standard locking pins. Once in place, it lies in the MRP gear cradles on the driver's right side. A full-length zipper keeps the fabric from flapping around during the ride, whether it be traversing rough terrain on the ATV or on a trailer-mounted 70-mile-per-hour blast down the highway to get from your home to your cabin. Once you arrive at your favorite spot, simply remove the cover and open the blind, right over the top of the ATV.

Once set up, the Rapid Blind's netting hides hunters from the game.

The Rapid Blind sets up in minutes and only takes a single person to accomplish the task.

Setup takes a few minutes. After unfolding the main structural support, snap six aluminum poles in place using nylon fittings. Installing the poles could not be easier; all locations are color coded, so it's simple and straightforward to set up. The main vertical supports are adjustable, so the blind can stand tall or be minimized for especially wary game. When extended to full height, the blind is 89 inches tall.

A large front panel door zips open for quick access in and out of the blind. For shooting, the roof zips open and rolls up out of the way. In its place, a camouflage net attaches with hook-and-loop fasteners, ready to be quickly pulled down when the birds fly in. The dark interior and camo netting make it difficult to see what's in the blind from a distance of more than 10 feet.

During our North Dakota snow goose hunt, the geese flew right to us, never suspecting that there were several hunters and an ATV in hiding. Snows are generally wary birds—the average age is 14 years — and they aren't dumb. Luckily, we held the advantage. When the birds flew into range, a simple yank on the net's rip strap gave us an open shooting lane.

**Left and top next page:**
From the inside, it's easy to see out, but from outside, it's nearly impossible to see in.

When the game is in range, pull down the netting and take aim. From completely concealed to shooting takes less than two seconds.

In addition to the large opening overhead, there are additional portholes for bow hunters or gun hunters working on big game, predators, or varmints. Each of the portholes zips open and can be covered with shoot-through net for total concealment.

Hunters should check state laws where they hunt for regulations on hunting near a vehicle. In Minnesota, where Arctic Cat is based, it is illegal to hunt from the seat of an ATV. However, it is legal to hunt standing next to a machine, provided no part of your body or firearm is in contact with the ATV.

The blind is available in two camo patterns: Mossy Oak Shadow Grass and Mossy Oak Breakup. A solid blue version called the Rapid Shack will also be available soon for ice-fishing applications. Also, don't be surprised if Arctic Cat releases a white version for snow geese soon. The unit is constructed from 400-denier

Folded, the blind rides perfectly on the MPR gear cradles.

Cordura nylon. Cordura is windproof and water resistant, along with being fire resistant and rotproof.

The blind is definitely a benefit on a cold day because it helps keep you toasty warm and out of the wind. Yet if the temperature is really bitter, you may want to use a small sunflower heater to warm the inside up significantly. A heater would be especially nice for ice fishing use.

The Rapid Blind sells for $650 in blue and $800 in camo. Though that's expensive compared to most pop-up hunting blinds, it is also larger than many blinds on the market and it completely conceals an ATV.

| PROJECT 23 | Hauling a Deer |
|---|---|

By Blake Stranz

**Time:** As much time as needed

**Tools:** Trailer, ATV

**Talent:** ★★

**Tab:** $450 for the Pak-Mule

**Parts:** A Pak-Mule or other trailer

**Tip:** Any ATV trailer will do

**Benefit:** Make hunting easier with a quick and small trailer

Most deer hunters will admit that they've overloaded their ATV racks to haul a trophy buck out of the woods. But despite the loss of handling and performance, few hunters like to use a trailer to get big game out of the woods. But using one might be the best option.

One trailer out on the market that is specifically designed with hunters in mind is the Pak-Mule from Summit Treestands. The Pak-Mule is unique because it can be hauled two ways. The first option is to simply couple the trailer to a 1 7/8-inch ball on an ATV and pull it around a hunting area. But if you appreciate your quad's maneuverability when not towing a trailer, the Pak-Mule folds and hangs on the rear rack of the ATV for greater convenience. Plus, the folding action allows the trailer to be hauled on the ATV even when it's loaded on a trailer or in the back of a pickup.

For greater maneuverability or transport in a pickup, the Pak-Mule can be carried on ATV racks.

## Start with Parts

The 80-pound trailer comes unassembled, but its instructions are simple to follow. It takes about an hour to assemble. Once the basic chassis of the trailer is built, buyers have to attach the axles and tires, shocks, hitch, and liner. A "tailgate" goes on the back when the Pak-Mule is in trailer mode and across the top for hauling on the ATV's rear racks. Hooks that attach to the ATV's rear rack hold the unit in place. The holes for the attachment points of the tailgate are not predrilled, making it difficult to get them perfectly lined up with an electric drill. The last step of the installation process is to affix the rack hooks to the ATV's rear rack with the supplied U-bolts.

## Rack 'Em

The Pak-Mule switches from trailer to rack-mount with little effort. First, pull the pins securing the tailgate and move it to its position across the top of the trailer. Reinsert the pins to secure it. Next, remove the large pin on the hitch bar to allow it to pivot. The Pak-Mule stays connected to the ball on the ATV the entire time. Pivot the unit up and hook it over the rack-mounted support arms. Then use the provided tie-downs to secure the trailer in the "up" position.

Pins secure the tilt mechanism on the tongue and move the tailgate for rack mounting.

Despite doubts, the Pak-Mule stayed on the rack hooks nicely, and the tie-down straps did an excellent job holding it in place. Modest bouncing has little effect on the stability of the unit, which means that it will work fine in the woods.

## Trailer Time

Once you've bagged that bruiser, reverse the straps and flip the trailer down onto its wheels. Use the straps to secure the trophy. The trailer holds 500 pounds and has shocks rated at 450 pounds. Air-filled tires track nicely and the shocks smooth out the ride. The shocks have preload adjustment that allows the suspension settings to match the weight in the trailer.

The Pak-Mule ($449) is made from green, powder-coated aluminum and has a black ABS plastic liner. These features allow the trailer to blend in when in the woods and simplify cleaning. Another plus for the Pak-Mule is that the trailer is only 32 inches wide, so it can squeeze through anything an ATV can.

As a trailer, the unit can haul 500 pounds, far more than the rack capacity on any ATV.

# PROJECT 24 | Planting a Food Plot

By Chaz Rice

**Time:** A few days

**Tools:** Plotmaster, seed, ATV

**Talent:** ★★★

**Tab:** Plotmaster starts at $2,195

**Tip:** Read up on what seeds to plant; different game snack on different plants

**Benefit:** Without food, there will be no game

Any hunter knows the value of a food plot. Anything to attract more harvestable animals is a plus in the world of hunting. If you are considering planting a food plot next season—or you're sick of the backbreaking work that is required to plant one—then this project is a must-read.

Plotmaster is a unique pull-behind ATV implement that makes the planting of a food plot possible in two swipes. Two swipes?! Well, not the whole plot, but a 48-inch-wide swath of it. The first pass plows and discs the land to break up the soil; the second plants the seed.

Sounds too good to be true, right? Well, read on.

**Left and previous page:** Planting is a snap with the user-friendly Plotmaster.

The Plotmaster comes in two platforms: electric lift and manual lift. We at *ATV Magazine* tested the electric lift and, judging from our experience, it is worth the extra money. Even though the electric motor raises and lowers the deck slowly, it is still faster and much easier than doing the same by hand. And this makes on-the-fly adjustments possible.

For the first step, you need to load your seed (we tested with clover) into the seed bin located on the back of the Plotmaster. A flip-top lid makes loading easy and clean. The seed spreader has two adjustments to maintain the delivery of seed. The first is a flap near where the seed exits the hopper. The second adjustment lets the user determine the seed fall rate via a five-position selector.

The Plotmaster does a great job of regulating seed delivery on smooth ground. On rough and rocky terrain, however, the unit bounces so much it is harder to get a proper seed spread. Then again, any unit smaller than a full-blown tractor would run into such problems in rocks.

Up front, the disc has three blade angle settings. Just select how much you want to break up the soil and adjust the angle as such. The sturdy discs break up the topsoil, even in extreme conditions. The ground we tested the unit on was rocky and the discs handled rocks with no problems. Sure, it wobbled around a little, but its hefty weight—Woods-N-Water recommends at least a 300-cc engine to pull the unit—made sure the Plotmaster tracked in the soil.

With a variety of attachments, the Plotmaster will work in different soil conditions for a number of duties.

Behind the discs are the plowing points that dig into the soil and weight the machine so the discs can properly break up the soil. Three different-sized plow points are available, and switching between them is not a problem.

To cover the planted seed, the Plotmaster comes with a cultipacker for smaller seeds and a drag for larger seeds. For clover, the cultipacker worked with great results. Whatever you choose, these are mounted on a 180-degree pivot point so they can swing away when not needed. The small clover seeds needed a little extra down-pressure to pack in properly, and the cultipacker is spring-loaded to facilitate this.

The platform unit comes complete with a disc harrow and attachments for a sweep plow, chisel plow, cultivator, electrical-seeded cultipacker, and drag. The fun doesn't stop there, however. The list includes 13 additional attachments and ranges from an aerator to a 15-gallon sprayer. If you need to do more than plant a plot on your land, chances are an attachment is available.

In all, the Plotmaster weighs 500 pounds. With seed, it probably weighs around 750 pounds. It is heavy, and you should make sure your ATV is ready to do the work. Automatic CVT-type ATVs could burn a belt, so make sure the ATV is in "low" gear.

The beautiful part of the Plotmaster is its ability to get way back where a tractor cannot. And this is where those big bucks roam! Deer like isolated spots. Before, if you wanted to plant seed on isolated land, it would take much more work. The Plotmaster simplifies the process so it's an essential addition to a hunting club's arsenal and equally important to the individual hunter.

Price for the manual lift is $2,195; an electric is $2,495. Attachments range between $145 and $895.

# PROJECT 25 | Goin' Ice Fishin'

By Chaz Rice

**Time:** 2 to 8 hours

**Talent:** ★

**Tab:** $50–$1,000

**Parts:** Ice fishing supplies

**Tip:** Have fun

**Benefit:** Catch fish with the ultimate ice fishing setup

Just west of Minneapolis, Minnesota, sits Lake Minnetonka. In the summer, the lake is full of pleasure cruisers, fishing boats, water skiers, personal watercraft, and sailboats. It is a playground for the people of the Twin Cities.

In the winter, when the cold sets to making ice, it turns into an ice fishing paradise. Some may think ice fishing is a crazy pastime for crazy people, but the diehard ice-fishing enthusiast doesn't mind when the naysayers stay home and watch the latest reality television show. The ice is better off without them!

There is something about sitting on an overturned bucket on the ice. A crystal-clear blue sky surrounds you, a perfect pair of sunglasses blocks the glare from the white snow and beautiful sun, brats are on the grill, the game is on the radio, and you just had a nibble on your line. Those Old Milwaukee commercials were right.

Arctic Cat's Rapid Shack makes a great mobile ice house for fishing. The shack sets up in minutes and is a shelter to stay warm in while on the ice. It is roomy too. The Rapid Shack can fit two people comfortably.

Ice fishing is clearly a northern pastime. In fact, all states with a passion for fishing and cold winters sustain a healthy number of diehard fishermen on the winter's ice. Minnesota is no different. On any free weekend, any true lover of the North Star State likes to fire up the auger and try his or her luck. Sometimes the fish cooperate, sometimes they don't. But you always manage to have a good time.

The key is preparation. No ice-fishing trip can start after 12 p.m. Nope, in order to outsmart the fish, you must get out on the ice and set up while the sun is rising. See, this reinforces the idea that we ice-fishing fiends are crazy. Loading up a truck in the freezing cold at 6 a.m. may make us feel tough, but to the rest of the world it makes us look like fools.

That's OK. The crazier we look, the fewer number of people will join us on the ice. Plus, if too many holes are drilled into the ice, the ice will end up sinking! That's another misconception we use to our advantage.

Second, you have to spend a lot of money on bait. Don't forget this important step. Too little bait and the battle is lost. Minnows, mealworms, etc.—these are all important aspects to the continuing battle between man and fish. Another important tip: Make sure to say, "I need a volunteer" when reaching into the minnow bucket. Again, we are looking for a convincing lunatic persona.

Third is food. Whatever you do, don't skimp on the meals. Even if you don't end up catching fish, make sure you remember the meal. A grill is a nice touch out on the ice. And no, it won't melt through. Beef jerky is a must too. We'll accept turkey jerky, but only under special circumstances. If you bring turkey jerky, make sure you have a good reason.

Fourth relates to "tip ups." In some states, like Minnesota, you can have two lines per person. One of these lines can be what is referred to as a tip up. This is a device that can be left unattended above a hole. The line from a tip up is attached to a baited hook and set to a permanent depth. The tip up is then left on its own and if a fish happens to hit the line, a flag is released on the tip up and everyone must yell "Tip up!"

The next step in the saga is optional. When a person goes to set the hook on the tripped tip up, someone must run at speed and tackle the target just before he gets to the device. This aids in camaraderie, but may also end in someone needing first aid.

Fifth? A good motorized ice auger is key. One with a 10-inch diameter is adequate. Less than that and you can't get those lunkers through the ice (uh-huh) and any larger and you are bound to twist an ankle stepping into a drilled hole!

Augers are always ornery after a season of heavy use. And since most ice fishing enthusiasts don't think about their auger until the night before the trip, it never idles properly.

The last one involves fish. Or, perhaps, no fish. Whether you catch fish is not the reason for getting out on the ice. Rather it is the experience. But bringing a load of fish home is good justification to any significant others. Just make sure you clean them first. And a good bottle of white wine makes a nice dinner. Hint, hint.

The Rapid Shack comes with a zippered boot to protect the Cordura fabric during transport.

Here is the Rapid Shack stored on the ATV. As you can see, it is quite compact.

## What about the ATVs?

Shouldn't this trip tie into ATVs somehow? After all, while fishing may not be our expertise at *ATV Magazine*, ATVs are. We had two ATVs along on this fishing trip. One was a Polaris Sportsman 700 Twin EFI, the other an Arctic Cat 650. Both were 2004 models, but one was specially rigged up for ice fishing.

The Arctic Cat was equipped with items from the company's multi-rack platform (MRP) ice fishing package. For those who aren't aware of the MRP system, it is a tool-less system allowing the ATV rider to equip the racks with a multitude of items specific to a job.

While some hardy fishermen drag permanent houses out to their favorite fishing spot, we prefer to remain mobile. That way, if we're not catching fish, we can move. It is a simple philosophy that works for both professional fishermen and our fathers, too.

This is why ATVs make the perfect ice fishing tools. What's more perfect is that Arctic Cat takes mobility to a new level with its Rapid Shack system. Basically this is a fire-resistant, canvas-like shelter that folds over the ATV in minutes and is made of sturdy, waterproof Cordura fabric. It is ingenious.

Instead of dragging a sled with the shelter behind the ATV, and thus slowing progress, a fisherman can quickly transport a shack using this system. In its collapsed state, it is relatively compact and stores nicely out of the way. It unfolds like a big blue oyster shell. The shack sweeps over the entire ATV, which acts as a good weight to prevent the shelter from blowing away. When collapsed, the shack also has a transport boot, which wraps around it to protect it from brush or other objects when the ATV is being pulled by a trailer.

Here is the Rapid Shack being deployed. Two people make it easier, but one person can deploy it too.

Once the shack is up, snap the reinforcing poles into place. These make the shack rigid enough to withstand strong winds.

Unfolding the shack is a fun experience, especially if there are spectators wondering what the heck you are doing. Yes, even crazy ice fishermen have the ability to think someone is nuts. Be prepared to be the envy of both your ice fishing buddies and ATV riding buddies. And if you have friends who do both, well, then you are touched by the ATV gods.

Aluminum poles form the study frame, and the shack has a large door for easy access. It even has a nice window to let light into the shack and zippered vents to let in fresh air.

Two adults can easily fit inside the shack and remain comfortable; three would work in a pinch. The Rapid Shack measures 88 inches x 89 inches x 100 inches.

Installation of the MRP package took a couple of hours when done at a leisurely pace. It helps to have someone to assist you. The hardest part was assembling the poles and keeping everything straight. We even had to drill a couple of holes that were mysteriously missing from two aluminum frame members. The directions insisted they should be there, and installation was halted until we drilled them. That was the only hangup of the entire installation since the directions were well written.

Stringing the poles through the blue shack material is easy. Everything is color coded so a mistake is hard to pull off. Again, you need someone else to help you with this installation—especially when assembling the shack over the ATV. The material is expensive and a rip during installation could easily ruin one's day.

At about $650, the shack is a big-ticket item. But it is comparable to other shacks on the market of the same size. Plus, you won't want to wait to use it again because it involves an ATV.

A bucket holder is a must when ice fishing. Arctic Cat makes one that plugs into its MRP system.

The ice auger is well proctected in Arctic Cat's auger holder. During a trip across the ice, the auger did not bounce much because of the rack holding the auger's power head.

We also tested Arctic Cat's auger holder. This piece consisted of a large-diameter plastic tube that mounts with straps to either the front or rear rack. Along with it was a rack that fits underneath the auger's power head for support. We chose to mount the holder on the front of the ATV so we could keep an eye on it while transporting across the lake. The auger holder retails for $120 and includes pads to help support the auger's power head.

Another neat addition for the ice fisherman is the MRP bucket holder. Any person who has gone ice fishing knows the need for a good five-gallon bucket. Whether it is holding gear or being used as a seat, the bucket is good. This sturdy holder secures most five-gallon buckets and holds them securely when driving across the ice. The bucket holder retails for $40.

Another useful item is the rack basket. Again, the MRP system makes it easy to install and remove.

Arctic Cat's backrest is just what our back needed after a long day of not catching fish. Shown in the background is Arctic Cat's MRP rack basket.

A useful accessory is Arctic Cat's fender bag. It comes in handy for holding all sorts of loose items and attaches quickly to the ATV's fender.

The basket is huge; it spans most of the rack. It can carry any loose items that you may need while on the ice. It can even hold a small cooler for beverages. The basket retails for $140, is made of high-gauge steel, and is powder-coated black.

And no long trip to a fishing destination is complete without a backrest. These handy items are just what you need after a day hunched over an ice hole waiting for the fish to bite. The backrest swivels up and down for comfort and is fully adjustable back and forward. It easily plugs into the MRP rack. The backrest sells for $100.

The final Arctic Cat–branded item was its fender bag. This bag came in handy for carrying smaller items such as a mini tackle box and a disposable camera for taking pictures of fish. The bag attaches to the fender with quick clips and hooks. Taking it off the fender is easy. The retail price of the fender bag is $45.

Since we were riding in the cold, we also mounted a pair of Kimpex's CKX Handlebar Mitts. These are one of the best ways to block cold winds from chilling your fingers. The mitts take a little getting used to, unless you are fully aware where the ATV controls are, but they do block the wind. They retail for $20.

These CKX-branded mitts from Kimpex can keep your hands warm while riding out to your fishing spot.

# Resources

**Project 1—Cleaning up Shop**
Pit Pal
(888) 748-7257
www.pitpal.com

Pour-N-Restore
(800) 508-7939
www.pour-n-restore.com

**Project 2—Working with an Air Lift**
Handy Industries
(800) 247-7594
www.handyindustries.com

**Project 3—Mounting & Inflating Tires**
Douglas Wheel Inc.
(760) 758-5560
www.douglaswheel.com/atv.htm

**Project 4—Choosing & Using a Mower**
Swisher Mower & Machine Company
(800) 222-8183
www.swisherinc.com

Kunz Engineering Inc.
(815) 539-6954
www.kunzeng.com

**Project 5—Plowing Soil**
Weekend Warrior
(866) 539-8944
www.weekend-warrior.com

**Project 6—Plowing Snow**
Cycle Country
(800) 841-2222
www.cyclecountry.com

Moose Utility
www.mooseutilities.com

Swisher Mower & Machine Company
(800) 222-8183
www.swisherinc.com

Warn
(800) 910-1122
www.warn.com

**Project 7—Adding Heated Grips**
Hot Grips, Dept. ATV
(603) 448-0303
www.hotgrips.com

**Project 8—Loading & Transporting ATVs**
ETEC (Environmental Technologies Equipment Corp.)
(800) 434-5309
www.etec.ca/atvlp.htm

TK Loader
(304) 257-5430
www.tkloader.com

Advanced Recreational Products, Dept. ATV
(888) 503-8855
www.arpatv.com

B & M Products
(888) 594-9910

Fulton Performance Products
(715) 693-1700
www.fultonperformance.com

**Project 9—Selecting the Right Transport Trailer**
Featherlite
(800) 870-1231
www.fthr.com

Pace American
(800) 247-5767
www.paceamerican.com

ShoreLand'r
(800) 859-3028
www.shorelandr.com

ThorCalifornia
(909) 697-4190
www.thorca.com

TPD
(916) 381-0532
www.tpdtrailers.com

Triton
(800) 232-3780
www.tritontrailers.com

Fleetwood RV
(800) 445-3307
www.fleetwoodrv.com

Carry-All
(770) 962-2724
www.carryallracks.com

**Project 10—Buying a Trailer or Rack Box**
Nordell Corporation
(800) 262-4129
www.nordell.com

Cycle Country
(800) 841-2222
www.cyclecountry.com

LMI Welding Inc.
(800) 345-5623
www.lmiwelding.com

**Project 12—Riding Safely**
ATV Safety Institute
(800) 887-2887
www.atvsafety.org

**Project 14—Using a Winch**
Warn Industries
(800) 910-1122
www.warn.com

Superwinch
(860) 928-7787
www.superwinch.com

**Project 15—Adding New Clutch Plates and Springs**
Clymer
(913) 541-8645
www.clymer.com

DP
(716) 681-8806
www.dp-brakes.com

**Project 18—Fixing a Flat Tire**
Safety Seal
(800) 888-9021
www.safetyseal.com

Stop & Go International
(815) 455-9080
www.stopngo.com

Genuine Innovations
(800) 340-1050
www.innovationsaz.com

Quad Boss
www.quadboss.com

**Project 19—Quieting a Big-Bore Beast**
Kolpin Outdoors Inc.
(877) 956-5746
www.atvstealthexhaust.com

**Project 20—Adding Cruise Control**
MotorCycle Setup Pty Ltd.
+61 (3) 9808 2804
www.mccruise.com

**Project 21—Using Security Locks**
Surelock Wheel-Lock, The Evolution 2000 lock
(716) 765-9282

Hitchin' Post
(800) 791-1333

Kryptonite locks
(800) 729-5625
www.kryptonitelock.com

Maximum Security LockDown
(800) 662-8628

**Project 22—Turning an ATV into a Portable Hunting Blind**
Artic Cat
www.arctic-cat.com or visit any Arctic Cat dealer

**Project 23—Hauling a Deer**
Summit Treestands
(256) 353-0634
www.summitstands.com

**Project 24—Planting a Food Plot**
Woods-N-Water
www.theplotmaster.com
(888) 440-9108

**Project 25—Goin' Ice Fishin'**
Artic Cat
www.arctic-cat.com or visit any Arctic Cat dealer

# Index

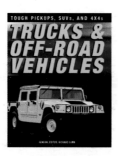
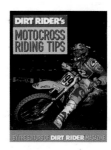

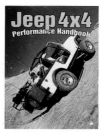